THE FALL
TO VIOLENCE

MARJORIE HEWITT SUCHOCKI

THE FALL TO VIOLENCE

ORIGINAL SIN
IN RELATIONAL THEOLOGY

CONTINUUM | NEW YORK

1995
The Continuum Publishing Company
370 Lexington Avenue, New York, NY 10017

Printed in the United States of America

Library of Congress Cataloging-in-Publication Data

Suchocki, Marjorie Hewitt.
  The fall to violence : original sin in relational theology /
Marjorie Hewitt Suchocki.
    p.   cm.
  ISBN 0-8264-0689-0 (hard : alk. paper)
  ISBN 0-8264-0860-5 (pbk.)
  1. Sin, Original. 2. Man (Theology) 3. Violence—Religious
aspects—Christianity. I. Title.
BT720.S83 1994
233'.14—dc20   94-21309
                                                              CIP

for
Catherine Faith Suchocki Orr

CONTENTS

ACKNOWLEDGMENTS

I am deeply grateful to the Board of Trustees at the School of Theology in Claremont for the sabbatical they granted me in the spring of 1992 for the purpose of developing the first draft of this manuscript. Thanks to the generous help of the Deutscher Akademischer Austauschdienst, I was able to spend that sabbatical in Heidelberg, Germany, where Professor Michael Welker and I team-taught a seminar on sin at the Theological Seminary of the University of Heidelberg. The stimulation of the seminar, plus many splendid conversations with Professor Welker and with students from the class, provided an ideal context in which to write the manuscript.

My work on this topic began early in 1989 following the catalyst of serving on a jury in Washington, D.C., as the preface will note in greater detail. Following that experience, I utilized the Georgia Harkness lecture at Garrett Evangelical Divinity School to begin my exploration of the topic of sin. This was followed in the next few years by lectures at St. Paul School of Theology, Wake Forest University, Louisville Presbyterian Seminary, the University of Alberta, the University of the South, Bethany College, Baldwin-Wallace College, and Hiram College. The United Methodist Church in Wenatchee, Washington, also provided an opportunity through their Albertson Lectures to develop material for the chapter on forgiveness. While there was some overlap between these various lectures, each series was quite different as I took advantage of the opportunities to explore the many nuances and problems entailed in the topic. The present volume goes beyond those lectures, but it would not exist without the background they provided.

I am also grateful to the students at my own schools, the School of Theology at Claremont and Claremont Graduate School, who studied the history of the doctrine of original sin in a seminar with me, and students at the Immaculate Heart College who spent a week working with me on the feminist dimensions of the doctrine of sin. And the Center for Process Studies gave me a forum for discussion of two chapters of the present work at afternoon seminars.

My faculty colleagues have inspired and helped me with their lively and insightful conversations. I am especially grateful to Jack Verheyden, Jack Coogan, Andrew Sung Park, Kathleen Greider, and Garth Baker-Fletcher. I am grateful to my two "croney" friends, Barbara Mitchell and Patricia McNaughton, whose spirited discussion and criticisms helped to clarify my project. And finally I express my gratitude to the best of editors, Justus George Lawler.

In Whitehead's memorable phrase, the many have become one—and are increased by one. My thanks to you all.

PREFACE

This book had its origins during a jury trial in Washington D.C. in the spring of 1989. I was Juror No. 1, serving somewhat grudgingly as we heard the evidence in a rather mundane drug case. After four days of testimony, we deliberated for six hours to bring in a unanimous verdict of guilty on all five counts as charged. I went home relieved that the chore was over, only to discover that in fact my "chore" was just beginning. For throughout the trial, issues and questions began their subliminal work within me, only to be raised to consciousness after the trial was over.

The sorry world of the crack house with its vials and white powders and guns had seemed so distant from my world as the academic dean of a theological seminary. But in truth, that "other" world was only a few miles from my home. Where did that world start, and where did it stop? "My" world was geographically close, but had I ever intentionally done anything at all to touch the lives in that "other" world? Was I only involved to judge its inhabitants? Or was there not a sense in which I was a participant in that world as well as mine, even if that participation were as an absentee neighbor?

I was well aware of the idealistic nature of my questions. The young defendant in the trial had given the impression of being a brutalized man; I would not want to walk the streets of his world alone at night. In his world, I have few survival skills.

Shortly thereafter I read of a young woman found shot to death in the small hours of the night in downtown D.C. She was a nineteen-year old prostitute who had run from an abusive home in Pennsylvania four years before her death. A pimp, waiting at the bus station for just such troubled youngsters as she, gave her "shelter" and a profession. The clients of the prostitute were the "johns"—suburban men who came to K Street by the busload after dark. She was bought and sold not once, but many times a night on the auction block of prostitution. This world, too, was but a few miles from my own. How was my world interwoven with this? Where does sin and guilt start, and where does it stop? How is it that so many webs of violence and violation are woven into our social structures, and if they are so woven, then do they not affect all who share in the society? Am I not also a participant in these structures, even through my passivity?

Both situations—the drug pushers and the prostitute—involved far more guilty parties than could be named at a trial. Economic structures, international policies, institutional racism, and illiteracy were ghostly witnesses to criminal formation at the trial. Sexism, condoning sexual violation and violence toward women and children both privately in "domestic affairs" and publicly in tacitly acceptable prostitution, had joined forces with that teen-ager's murderers long years before the trigger was pulled. All persons within society participate to some degree in the society's economic structures, international policies, racism, and sexism. Where does sin start and stop; where does guilt start and stop? And are there conditions that orient us toward sin?

The ancient church developed a notion of "original sin," clothed in mythic structures, that spoke to conditions set in force long before our individual births that nonetheless orient each of us toward sin. The notion carried conviction for more than a millennium of Christian history, but lost ground in the age of the Enlightenment. We now live in a world deeply attuned to the extensiveness and intensiveness of relationality. And so I began to muse on the possibilities of relational theology to reappropriate the powerful notion of original sin.

Through four years of research, teaching, and lecturing, I have developed the theses represented in the nine chapters of this book. First, my working definition of sin is participation through intent or act in unnecessary violence that contributes to the ill-being of any aspect of earth or its inhabitants. In the first chapter I contrast this with the meaning of original sin as developed by Augustine in the early church, and by Reinhold Niebuhr in the twentieth century. For both Augustine and Niebuhr, sin is rebellion against God through the sin of pride. I present my reasons for rejecting their definition, and in the second chapter develop the notion of sin as rebellion against creation through unnecessary violence.

In rejecting the primary definition of sin as rebellion against God, I do not thereby assume that sin has no effect on God. Quite to the contrary; in a process-relational world, it is impossible for God *not* to be affected by that which happens in the world, be it sin or saintliness. Therefore, in my third chapter I show how a primary understanding of sin as rebellion against creation entails sin against God as well. I see this as a reversal of the tradition: rather than rebellion against God being the primary sin that engenders all others, I see rebellion against creation as the fundamental sin. Since God must experience the world, violence in creation also entails violence against God.

In chapter four I deal with a problem entailed by the reversal of sin's primary target. If sin is rebellion against God, then that which is against God's will is sin. But if sin is rebellion against creation, what constitutes the criterion that marks sin as sin? My answer is that absence of well-being is the criterion, and I develop what this means in a relational world.

If chapters one through four establish sin as a violation of well-being entailing violence against creation and against God, the major question is still the one dealt with by the tradition: why? Why is violation and violence so universally human? In chapters five through seven I develop a tripartite analysis of original sin. Chapter five argues that a bent toward violence is woven into the fabric of our humanity. In chapter six I argue that because all aspects of the world are united through interrelationality, whereby each receives from all and gives for all, all inherit from each other's sins. Thus the solidarity of the race exacerbates the condition of sin created through our bent toward violence. In chapter seven I present the thesis that sin is also exacerbated by inherited norms of ill-being that guard the privilege of the few at the expense of the many.

Thus the trifold structure of sin is a bent toward violence through our evolution, the interwoven relationality that creates a solidarity to the human race, and the temporal structures of intersubjectivity through which we inherit assumptions concerning how we interpret, value, and act in our world. Insofar as these presuppose the ill-being of any aspect of creation, then we are involved in support and perpetuation of that ill-being. We are sinners.

In the eighth chapter I ask the question: If these structures of sin affect us simply through our being human, why name the situation as sin? Sin implies responsibility; in what way are we responsible? This, of course, is the question of guilt, and the question of guilt simultaneously involves the question of freedom. To the degree that the capacity for transcendence is present in any act or intent toward unnecessary violence, then to that degree there is freedom, guilt, and responsibility.

Thus I have reappropriated the ancient doctrine of original sin, albeit it in a relational world where its fundamental nature is measured by the degree to which it contributes to unnecessary violence against creation. As a Christian theologian, I cannot responsibly halt my investigation here. Sin and guilt require an answer, and I see that answer resting in the hope and act of forgiveness. Therefore in my final chapter I have developed a notion of forgiveness that corresponds to the understanding of sin. To forgive is to will the well-being of victim and violator in the fullest possible knowledge of the nature of the violation. Forgiveness, then, is the exercise of transcendence through memory, empathy and imagination; it is the hope of our humanity, since it wields the power to break the cycles of violence. The event of forgiveness is a lifetime investment in naming ourselves and each other as we are and as we can be in the continuing evolution of our humanity.

I began my reflections on this book through contact with the harshness of violence, and the awareness that we all participate in and share responsibility for that violence. Theological reflection on violence can in fact do violence to experience by rationalizing away its surd quality, and smoothing its terror-stricken edges with a fine turn of phrase. I have chosen to begin each chapter with a stark description of sin given in the impersonal language of a news report. In some chapters I attempt to measure my thinking against the description given; in other cases, it simply stands as a reminder of the irreducibility of violence. Our theologies cannot render it rational. What they can do is point to our joint responsibility, and name the power of God through and for forgiveness and transformation.

SIN

The United States, from its biggest cities to its smallest towns, is an increasingly violent place to be a woman—one of the most violent in the world.

Exactly how violent is hard to measure. In the official census of crime in this country, the FBI tracks rape but not domestic violence. Studies to gauge the problem, however, demonstrate that there is no right to be female in America and be safe.

Certainly this is a dangerous country for everyone. At current crime rates, 89 percent of men and 73 percent of women will be victims of violence at least once in their lives, a 1987 Justice Department study found. But women are six times more likely than men to be attacked by someone they know. Once every 15 seconds in the United States a woman is beaten by her husband or boyfriend. One of every eight women—at least 12.1 million—has been raped sometime during her life, according to a 1992 nationwide survey by the National Victim Center in Fort Worth. The FBI says 106,000 rapes were reported in 1991, but law enforcement officials say police are not called in most rapes. Violence is the prime cause of injuries to women ages 15 to 44, more common than auto accidents, muggings, and cancer combined, according to the U.S. surgeon general. The perpetrators overwhelmingly are male.

—Dallas Morning News
Sunday, June 6, 1993

PART 1
THEOLOGICAL FOUNDATIONS OF SIN

CHAPTER
1

ORIGINAL SIN

S in has been considered primarily as rebellion against God throughout most of Christian history. However, in this book I propose a new definition: Sin as the violence of rebellion against creation. Sin is unnecessary violence against any aspect of existence, whether through act or intent, whether consciously chosen or otherwise. Sin is the violation of creation, and therefore a rebellion against creation's well-being. Insofar as creation involves God as creator, sin also entails a violation against God. But sin is defined primarily from the perspective of its relation to creation, whether self or others, and only secondarily defined in terms of its relation to God. Sin is first and foremost a rebellion against creation.

Like the traditional notion of sin as rebellion against God, the proposed notion of sin as rebellion against creation is intended as a root concept, underlying and illuminating all the various forms of actual sin. Therefore, it is a revision of the ancient concept of original sin. That concept defined the plight of every human being in several ways: First, it was a condition generated by the presumed first parents of the human race; second, it was an inherited condition that predisposed each and every human being to sinful acts; and third, it plunged every human being into a condition of guilt. Thus under the original concept of original sin, to exist is to be born into a situation where, whether one wills it or not, one will be implicated in a rebellion against God. The revised notion of original sin as rebellion against creation will retain the dire seriousness involved in the original concept, but in radically different ways.

To revise the concept of sin from rebellion against God to rebellion against creation entails certain problems. 1) Since Christian theologians have traditionally defined sin in terms of pride or its corollary, unbelief, and therefore as rebellion against God, how can we justify reversing the definition by understanding sin primarily in connection with creaturely relationships? 2) If the tradition interprets "rebellion against God" as being a rebellion precisely because it involves misuse of creaturely existence, what is the value of replacing "rebellion against God" with "rebellion against creation"? Do they not mean essentially the same thing in the tradition? And do we not risk losing the important God-reference altogether by turning the focus toward creation? 3) If such questions could be raised by a theologian, a secularist might well raise yet another kind of objection relative to the word "creation." Why not simply use the word "existence"? What is properly added to the given definition by calling it a rebellion against "creation"? Is it possible thoroughly to secularize the concept of sin?

I will be addressing such questions throughout this treatment of sin as violence. My argument is that neither the traditional definition of sin as a rebellion against God nor its corollary concept of original sin as rooted solely in human freedom is adequate to account for the enormity and variety of ways by which we manage to inflict ill-being upon ourselves, one another, and our environing earth. The difficulties with interpreting sin as a rebellion against God are several.

First, the concept of sin as rebellion against God tends to cast the primary function of God as the moral lawgiver who establishes the boundaries of acceptable human conduct. This is accompanied by an image of human nature that already exceeds those boundaries, so that God the moral lawgiver is also God the judge. God the Redeemer corrects the situation, so that humans are theoretically empowered to stay within the divinely set boundaries, which often turn out to be the cultural mores of a particular society. But perhaps staying within arbitrarily or culturally defined boundaries is not the fundamental problem of the human condition, in which case the notion of God that is tied to such an interpretation is part of the problem rather than part of the solution.

Second, and related to the above, to call all sin a rebellion against God too easily translates into a social formula for keeping marginalized and oppressed peoples in places of poverty and/or powerlessness, since it tends to interpret rebellion against any form of political, social, or personal power as a rebellion against God.

Third, to hide all sin, whether the enormity of political torture, massive wars, cruel oppressions, child abuse, or more idiosyncratic personal sins, under the one umbrella of rebellion against God effectively levels the distinction between sins.

Fourth, it also renders invisible the very real and often intended victims of sin. This adds to the violation of these victims, and hence increases rather than explains the sins from which they suffer.

Fifth, it contributes to the devaluation of creation. It depends upon a hierarchical view that posits creation as lower than humankind, God above humankind, and humans somewhere in the midst. Since rebellion is against that which is over one, sin as rebellion must be against God rather than creation. But naming sin as rebellion against God rather than creation implies that creation in and of itself is not significant enough that crimes directly intended against its well-being should merit the name of sin. Such a view itself displays the sin of arrogance, and hides the identity of humanity as a full part of creation.

Sixth, the concept actually fosters rather than illumines the Christian problem of sin. By isolating the individual from the rest of creation, as such a concept does, it already suggests a godlike aspect to humanity. To cast the human in such a role gives a larger-than-life position to the human that suggests the very self-deification it condemns. To this extent, this description of sin becomes an invitation to sin.

Seventh, sin as rebellion against God makes the fundamental conflict of human beings a promethean defiance of deity which is probably remote from the experience of most people. This is particularly so in a largely secular society, where the notion of God is often confined to expletive use, and where there is only vague consensus as to the existence or the nature of God. One must do mental gymnastics with the concept of rebellion against God to apply it to most of the deeds of ill-doing in the world today, where rebelling against God or being god-like is often irrelevant to the consciousness or intentions of most perpetrators of evil. While it is true that the Christian theologian can perform the necessary translation so as to recast evil deeds into the conceptuality of rebellion against God, it is time once again to employ Ockham's razor with a more direct description of sin as a rebellion against the well-being of creation. To be sure, to move in such a direction raises the issue of the criterion of well-being, a criterion presumably addressed in the earlier notion of rebellion against God. If rebellion against God is the primal sin, then the criterion of sin is whatever goes against the command of God—assuming, of course, that the human interpreters of the command of God have not injected their own best interests into the clarity of the command. By shifting the definition to rebellion against creation, the issue of what constitutes the well-being of creation enters into the picture anew. However, the meaning or application of the command to love God and neighbor has always required interpretation. The criteria by which we make such interpretations have always been embedded in the world. Thus, changing our definition of sin from a rebellion against God to a rebellion against creation does not introduce a new problem of criteria; it simply reveals an older and more hidden problem.

All of these issues must be clarified by going deeper into precisely what sin as rebellion against God meant in the Christian tradition. As with so many doctrines, the doctrine of sin has its formative expression in the work of Augustine, who drew upon the biblical understanding of his day, the accumulated theological wisdom of the early church, and of course upon his philosophical and cultural heritage. His fundamental teaching on sin might be best captured in his phrase, "All evil is the result of sin and its punishment."[1] He developed his understanding of the basis of sin through a mythic structure that powerfully captured his insight into the human condition.

Perhaps borrowing from earlier Gnostic and apocalyptic myths as well as his own Manichaean past, Augustine rooted sin not simply in human rebellion against God, but in a heavenly conflict prior to the creation of earth. Angelic beings, created for the purpose of praising God and enjoying the bliss of such praise forever, turned from their necessarily total dependence upon God to rely on their own created capacities instead. While such a story is simple, it contains profound depths. First, the praise of God *is* bliss because through praise, the beings are actively and positively participating in the divine being that is their very source of life. To praise God is in some sense to know God, but to know God is to know and be connected to the source of one's being, and therefore one's bliss. Thus the praise rendered to God in the story is not to be interpreted as some sort of flattery needed by the divine ego; to the

---

[1] Augustine, *On True Religion*, XII.23. The following summary of Augustine's position is drawn compositely from *City of God*, Books 11 through 14, *On the Freedom of the Will*, *On the Deserving of Sinners and their Forgiveness*, and *On Rebuke and Grace*, particularly Books X and XI.

contrary, it conveys the very graciousness and generosity of God as the sustainer of creation. The projected angelic turning from dependence upon God, then, is a turning not only from the source of bliss, but from the sustenance of being. Thus these angels "fall." But where is there to fall? There is the hint within the Christian myth of the gnostic and pagan versions that relate the creation of the visible universe to the consequences of the fall. God is invisible, immortal: the world is visible and most mortal. Its distance from God, then, is like the distance of the fall.

But such gnostic conclusions to the myth contradicted the goodness of the created order held through the Biblical witness. Hence Augustine did not incorporate these implications of the myth into his own developing doctrine of sin. Instead, by using the heavenly fall as a background he was able to set the stage for the human repetition of the angelic sin. He gave expression to the human experience that sin is somehow already a given, waiting at the door, and that this givenness of sin as a corrupting influence must be presupposed in the human situation.

The human is made in the image of God, by which Augustine meant the faculties of the soul insofar as these faculties are capable of knowing God. Remembering the role of the knowledge and praise of God for the angels, the human capacity also to know God speaks of the possibility of bliss and fulfillment for the human order, as it did for the angelic order. Being made in the image of God is precisely the avenue whereby the image can know its model, the creature its Creator, and thus enter into the praise and bliss of sustaining communion with God. Obedience in such a setting is neither hardship nor a contradiction to the created human nature; to the contrary, it is the fulfillment of human nature, establishing a communion with God that issues into social communion with one another, and harmonious communion with the rest of the created order. The Edenic pair, trusting in God and enjoying their natural state, begin existence, like the angels, in the bliss of obedience. And so was set the stage of the human drama patterned after the angelic drama: the creatures, being in the image of God, are sustained through the knowledge and praise of God. Their continuation in this bliss is dependent upon their own unbroken willingness to depend upon God.

The story follows its fated end: tempted by the already fallen angel—the predisposing sin—the human pair use their powers of self-transcendence not to contemplate the glory and wisdom of

God, but to question the limits of their own existence as decreed by God. To question limits which God has set is to make oneself the definer of one's own limits, which of course is to assume the prerogative of God the creator. It is, then, an effective rebellion against God, an insurrection that unseats God from the place of ruling one's life in favor of self rule.

Almost by definition, such prideful rebellion has a disastrous effect upon the image of God that is the sign of one's created ability for self-transcendence and communion with God. To turn from God to self is to turn from the source of one's life to that which cannot long sustain itself. To use a most contemporary metaphor, it would be like pulling the plug on an instrument that is also battery-operated: the instrument will continue to function for as long as the batteries last, but having lost its continuous source of power, the instrument will cease to function when its batteries inevitably give out. The creature who turns from its source to itself has turned from life to death. So Augustine interpreted the result of the fall.

Furthermore, since this rebellion against God consisted in the desire to transcend one's creaturely limits and be like God, then pride is the overarching definition of the creature with the now distorted image of God. Pride *is* rebellion against God, and hence the primal sin. This pride is not a single action, contained within the turn from God, but is rather both the initial action and its effects. Pride permeates the being of the rebellious creature, affecting every act, so that every act is an act tainted by sin. Augustine most consistently refers to this in terms of the turned will. That is, the human ability to transcend the self and commune with God is twisted and distorted within the depths of the self's freedom. Insofar as this freedom is the will of the creature, the will is defective. The creature, permeated by pride, is no longer capable of exercising the original communion with God. A prideful lust for created things in and for themselves, a darkened understanding with regard to the true knowledge of God, self, or world, and the invariable movement from birth toward death henceforth mark all human life.

Augustine completed the story of this rebellion by making it every individual's story. He accomplished this by developing several accounts of the transmission of sin from Adam and Eve to all their descendants. In *City of God*, he utilized the biology of his day. He understood all of Adam's progeny to be present within Adam's semen, so that as pride permeated and distorted Adam's entire being, it also distorted his semen, and so his descendants. Born of a twisted will, we are therefore twisted ourselves, and suffer from the distortions of a good creation now bent to evil ends. His other approach is typified in his treatise in *Against Julian*, where the transmission of original sin is through sexual intercourse. Augustine argued that Christ was born free of original sin precisely because there was no carnal intercourse involved in his conception. Here he built upon his understanding that a major consequence of the Adamic fall is that lust marks every human action, with lust being the desire for finite things in and of themselves, apart from reference to God. This reference to God is not arbitrary, since reliance upon God was the means of establishing communion not only with God, but also with all the created order. Lust is the distortion of this initial good, and Augustine considers lust most obviously present in sexual intercourse. Since all human progeneration occurs through sexual intercourse, the beginning of every human being is in and through lust; this beginning taints the nascent person so that it, too, is born with a bent toward lust. In both versions, the sensitivity is communicated that sin precedes us insofar as it has already corrupted us without our individually conscious consent. But being born a sinner, we quickly learn the ways of sin, adding our own contributions to the sorry history of this world. Having rebelled against God, we vent our ill upon a good creation that we no longer know how to use rightly.

The mythic structure of the story of human rebellion against God must not be allowed to mask the effectiveness of its description of the human plight. In Augustine's own time, and in the intervening centuries insofar as they shared a worldview that posited the historicity of a first pair, there was much heuristic value to the story. Against the biblical witness that God created the world good, every generation experiences the massiveness of human suffering, and the pervasiveness of wrongdoing. The senselessness often attendant upon both only increases the problem. How is the experience of suffering, ill-doing, and meaninglessness to be reconciled with the conviction that the world is the good creation of a good God? The Christian resolution codified in Augustine's reworking of Christian, Jewish, and pagan myths offered a coherence otherwise lacking to the world. Insofar as all persons, even the apparently innocent, could be associated with sin, and insofar as suffering could be interpreted as the natural consequence of a humanity no longer capable in its own strength of living from a full dependence upon God, then the human plight could be rendered at least intelligible. The rationality of the answer addressed the irrationality of sin and evil, providing Christians with a way to endure suffering and to contribute to the building of good. The Augustinian development of original sin as a prideful rebellion against God, affecting all humanity with vice, provided the parameters for a profound appropriation of Christianity.

Throughout Christian history this notion of sin as a prideful rebellion against God was adjusted to the various suppositions of each age. The distinctive Reformation variation was its emphasis upon unbelief rather than pride as the core sin, but since unbelief engendered pride, and since Augustine, too, spoke of the failure of the first pair to believe God, the Reformers stayed within the fundamental framework of the Augustinian structure. By failing to believe God's word of warning, which was also a word of enablement, Adam and Eve failed to rely on their source of life, and hence fell into sin and death for themselves and all their progeny. They rebelled against God, and with them, so do we.

With the erosion of the mythical aspects of the Augustinian representation of sin as rebellion against God—an erosion begun in the Renaissance and completed in the Enlightenment—Christian theology has been hard pressed to retain the explanatory notion of original sin as the presupposition of the human condition. The issue is difficult: How does theology retain some explanation for the pervasiveness of sin, and yet at the same time avoid implicating God as creator of an imperfect creation? Human freedom alone cannot bear the burden, for if the human will were in fact entirely free, then only some as opposed to all would sin. What accounts for the universality of sin, if there is no catastrophic rebellion on the part of a first pair?

The tendency has been so to define the human personality that it contains the predisposition but not the necessity of sin. Immanuel Kant, in *Religion Within the Limits of Reason Alone*, was the first modern thinker to analyze human evil in such a way, but twentieth century theology, with its new access to psychological structures of the human personality, was quick to follow suit. In thinkers such as Paul Tillich and Reinhold Niebuhr, the fragility of the human situation is such that it necessarily engenders anxiety, and this anxiety is the condition from which one actualizes sin. Since the antithesis of sin is to trust God despite one's anxiety, the religious dimension of sin is still cast as a primary rebellion against God. I turn now to a discussion of Reinhold Niebuhr's interpretation of sin to show its fundamental continuity with the Augustinian paradigm, despite its displacement of myth by psychology.[2]

Niebuhr recognized that the present age no longer has the same access to the Adamic myth that qualified so much of Christian history. But he, as much as his forebears, had to account for the pervasiveness of suffering and evil-doing, and to do so he recast the message within the Augustinian myth into a form no longer dependent upon a first pair or an angelic creation. In the first volume of *The Nature and Destiny of Man*, Niebuhr translated the Augustinian rebellion against God into an existential rebellion arising out of the human condition for every human individual.[3]

Niebuhr's anthropological assumptions are important in this task. Throughout all of his writings there is a consistent analysis of human existence as partaking of nature and spirit in an integrated unity. "Nature" is that aspect of our existence which we hold in common with other animals—our embodiedness, our appetites, our mortality. "Spirit," however, is directly continuous with an Augustinian interpretation of the "image of God." Spirit is that aspect of humanity that is capable of transcending itself. Niebuhr understood this transcendence to be dyadic, with a reference point to nature and to God. With regard to nature, the point of transcendence is the human mind itself. One doesn't simply think; one reflects upon one's thinking, questioning it, probing it—and thus transcending it. We think—and reflect upon our thought; we act—and reflect upon our actions. Furthermore, this capacity for self-transcendence is more than a faculty exercised with reference to the various moments of our lives, it is a capacity to consider the totality of our lives. We are—and we reflect upon the significance of our very

---

[2] Niebuhr is not alone among twentieth century theologians who account for the pervasiveness of evil by relating it to existential anxiety. Paul Tillich's account of the ambiguity and fragmentary nature of existence per se likewise points to anxiety as the condition from which sin arises. And even Karl Barth, who sees sin as humankind's no to God, explains the mystery of that "no" through the nothingness and attendant anxiety that pervade creaturely existence. While liberation theologians name sin as oppression, the root of this sin either is unexplored, or remains as the traditional pride with the twentieth century overtones of anxiety. In the most extended feminist treatment of sin, Judith Plaskow's *Sex, Sin, and Grace*, Niebuhr's analysis of anxiety as the root of sin is accepted, and his conclusions are expanded, as will be explored more fully in the following chapter. Thus the movement from a historical to a psychological account of sin is a wide enough phenomenon that Niebuhr can be used representatively for a twentieth century doctrine of original sin.

[3] Reinhold Niebuhr, *The Nature and Destiny of Man*, Volume 1 (New York: Charles Scribner's Sons, 1941, 1964).

being, not only in terms of our individual lives, but in terms of our place in the wider scheme of existence as a whole. In this ability to question existence as a whole, we establish ourselves as beings who transcend not only ourselves, but existence per se. We are peculiar creatures with the capacity to lift up our heads from the endless immersion in doing, thinking, and being, and to bring all things into question. This capacity constitutes our fundamental being as spirit.

But if our existence as spirit is the ability to transcend not only self, but existence per se, then our existence as spirit points beyond existence to another reality—and this is God. Niebuhr extensively quotes Augustine's reflections on memory from Book X of the *Confessions* to establish the link between his own understanding of human self-transcendence as spirit, and Augustine's reflections on the same topic. He understands Augustine as discovering that "the limits of the self lie finally outside the self," and that in fact "the human spirit in its depth and height reaches into eternity and that this vertical dimension is more important for the understanding of man than merely his rational capacity for forming general concepts. This latter capacity is derived from the former. It is, as it were, a capacity for horizontal perspectives over the wide world, made possible by the height at which the human spirit is able to survey the scene."[4] This height is none other than the human capacity to know God. Niebuhr recoils from making this capacity the basis for any mystical union with God, which would seem to him to be a self-deification of one's own consciousness. But this other side of self-transcendence is in fact the capacity that reaches into eternity, and is the ground of the spirit's ability to transcend not only self, but world.

Niebuhr gives by far the greater portion of his analysis of existence to an analysis of self-transcendence, but he has no intention of positing a bi-partite being of nature and spirit mysteriously held together without any admixture of the parts. One's spiritual component thoroughly qualifies one's natural aspects, transforming them with the power of self-transcendence, which translates to a measure of freedom. The infinite possibilities of the spirit transform every natural human function, making one's very embodiment a possible vehicle of spirit in the world. But spirit not only qualifies nature; nature qualifies spirit. The human spirit is finite, so that even its capacity for God is limited by the particularity of the self. A mystical

---

[4] Ibid., p. 156.

sense of total identity with God must be false, given this inexorable finitude of the human spirit. The natural aspect of human identity deeply touches and qualifies spirit. Nature and spirit exist in a dyadic unity, forming the fullness of human nature.

This summary of Niebuhr's anthropology is necessary in order to appreciate his appropriation of the notion of rebellion against God as the primary definition of sin. Since finitude qualifies the freedom of the spirit, and the freedom of the spirit qualifies our every finite capacity, humankind exists with a peculiar tension. Now following Søren Kierkegaard, Niebuhr posits that the tension entailed in our very uniqueness produces a natural anxiety over one's insecurity. Were we simply nature, we would be immersed in the things of nature with never a qualm, as Niebuhr presumes is the case with animals. But the infusion of freedom into nature raises the wider perspective of knowing our transience, our movement toward death, and hence our lack of security in the things of nature. We know anxiety. Likewise with spirit: Were we only spirit, we would soar, unlimited by the qualifications of perspective and self-interest that permeate spirit as a result of our finitude, our being as nature. We are limited as spirit, but those limitations are themselves bounded in the ambiguities provided through nature. How are we to accept and secure the proper limitations of spirit? And so our situation as beings composed of nature and spirit together is a situation of natural anxiety. Out of this anxiety comes the inevitable attempt to secure ourselves, which leads to sin. Sin can take the avenue of the spirit, in which case it is the setting up of oneself as one's own arbiter, defining limits and securing the self as if one's own limited perspective were in fact absolute. This is the sin of pride, whereby one ignores the finitude provided through nature. Alternatively, sin can take the avenue of nature, wherein one attempts to secure oneself by ignoring the freedom conferred upon nature through spirituality. The self hides from itself by giving itself over to whatever natural processes are at hand. This is the sin of sensuousness. Both are fundamentally sins against God, who sets one's limits, and therefore both are a rebellion against God.

Niebuhr's reason for naming the attempt to secure oneself, whether through spirit or through nature, as the primal sin is because there exists for us a given establishment of our limits and our security in God. The knowledge of this is mediated through general and special revelation, so that all persons theoretically have the resources to respond to anxiety by trusting in God, and hence avoiding sin. The fact that no one ever has or ever will avail oneself of this possibility and thus avoid sin entirely does not mean, for Niebuhr, that sin is necessary, only that it is inevitable. The difference is not always immediately obvious, but it is important for Niebuhr since any necessity to sin within human nature would mitigate human responsibility, and indeed, would implicate God as creator.

Niebuhr has succeeded in recreating for every individual a situation that parallels the dynamics and the tension held within the Augustinian myth of Adamic and angelic sin. Whereas Augustine located rebellion against God in the mythic histories of angels and a first human pair, and only consequently in all others, Niebuhr locates his very similar rebellion directly within each human personality. Adam is a symbolic rather than historical figure for Niebuhr. The mystery of sin, then, is rooted not in prehistory, but in a presupposition within personality.[5] The creature is limited and insecure in its own self; its security lies in its ability to trust God. By trusting God, the creature will find not only its security, but its bliss; by looking instead to its own resources, it leaves the source of its life and joins the sad history of the race in its hopeless attempt to ground itself, which is sin. All sin stems from this existential dynamic encountered by every human being; this is the original condition of sin, and hence Niebuhr's definition of original sin. And original sin is rebellion against God.

Niebuhr was notably astute in describing the daily personal and social sins of humankind. His profound analysis of the misuse of human power for social and personal ends is one of the monumental accomplishments in twentieth century theological ethics. But no matter how mundane the sin he was describing, or what psychological/sociological tools he incorporated into his analysis, he considered that the fundamental religious dimension of every sin was that outlined above as a primal rebellion against God.

Sin as rebellion against God, or pride, is thus well-established within the Christian tradition, whether one looks at the most significant of the patristic theologians, or to a major twentieth century figure. As demonstrated through Niebuhr, the contemporary defense of this interpretation of sin depends upon an ability to transpose the Adamic myth from the presumed historical origins of the

---

[5] Here there are many analogies with Immanuel Kant's work in *Religion Within the Limits of Reason Alone*, where Kant, too, accounted for sin through what he called the predisposition to personality within the structure of human existence.

species to the dynamics of existence per se, albeit by walking the fine if not impossible line of making a distinction between inevitable versus necessary sin. But hidden within this attempt are the very reasons for reversing the tradition, making rebellion against creation the primal sin, from which sin against God as creator is a derivative and therefore secondary form of sin.

This chapter was prefaced, as will be each chapter in this book, with an illustration of sin drawn from a public report. The reasons for including these accounts are multiple. First, to attempt to give an account of sin is to attempt to render rational that which defies rationality. There is a surd quality to human brutality and to our penchant for violence. By including actual reports of sin, I will insure that the raw reality of sin will not be bypassed in the attempt to give an account of sin.

Second, the secularization of American culture has contributed to the trivialization of sin. Such things as "going off one's diet," or "telling a white lie," constitute the "sins" that we name in our society. Such trivialization serves to hide the enormity of sin—to draw from a biblical image, we pick at motes, and ignore gigantic logs. The reports of sin introducing each chapter call us to face the gravity of the problem of sin.

In a similar vein, we too often treat sin as if it were synonymous with sex. The church's association of lust with original sin surely bears some of the responsibility for this, but no theologian of the church ever intended sexuality to be the summary of all lust. Yet today the mention of sin often elicits a knowing smile, as if the real topic were some form of sexuality. The illustrations of sin should disabuse us of such escapism.

Finally, the accounts can serve my arguments by being critical illustrations of sin. The empirical account can provide a ground for testing the intellectual account that names such realities as "sin." Is the theory adequate to the experience? While I work to develop an understanding of sin out of the experience of sin, I am convinced that no account of sin, and certainly not my own, is fully adequate to the awful reality of human ill-doing. The critical illustrations keep this inadequacy vividly before us.

The dire account of violence in the United States, particularly toward women, that begins this chapter and this book holds Augustine and Niebuhr as well as myself to account. Can such violence be encompassed by the analytical doctrines of sin typified in this chapter by Augustine and Niebuhr? To a woman, it seems a strange understanding of God that roots sin as violence, whether against women or others, in the desire to be like God, even if that desire is judged as doomed to failure. Likewise, pride and/or existential anxiety seem stretched to address the scope and intensity of such violence. Yet this instinctive response is too facile a dismissal of Augustine's and Niebuhr's accounts.

Both Augustine and Niebuhr would insist that in its religious depths, the violence named in this report stems from pride. Religiously, this pride is the inherent desire within fallen humanity to be like God, not in terms of character, but in terms of power. This, in turn, is exercised most fully in the power to define one's own limits. Violence against others could then be seen as fury concerning another's trespassing of one's own chosen sphere. Its nature as sin is in and through the fundamental usurpation of God's role as the one who decrees all limits. The usurpation is not necessarily conscious, nor does it have to be. Since God is the only proper determiner of one's place and conduct, actions that trespass God's will are by definition sin, and more specifically, the sin of pride. Thus the violence recounted in the report is sin because its foundations rest in the defiance of limits set by God, and hence in defiance of God.

While this theological use of sin as pride or anxiety surely bespeaks a world radically awry, there is an indirectness between the theological account and the raw material of human evil. The account makes violence the effect of a more primal sin. But could we not explore violence itself as that more primal sin? This has surely been done before: Freud in *Moses and Monotheism* and *Totem and Taboo* speaks of a primal murder, as does his more recent follower, René Girard. But my intent is not to posit an original violent act, which in effect follows the same dynamics as looking for an original Adam and Eve. Rather, it may be that violence itself is root as well as effect of sin. If this is so, then the news report of violence can be taken as a depiction of sin not because it is against limits set by God, but because violence is itself the root of sin since it by definition destroys well-being. Unnecessary violence is then the act of sin. Its transmission is through inherited inclination and socially inculcated habits, and its pervasiveness draws from the deep interrelationality of the human race.

But before I can develop these themes more fully, I must continue the argument that sin is the violation of creation, and therefore a rebellion against creation's well-being.

SIN

First, there was terror. One man in his sixties described how he watched the town's veterinarian, a Muslim, being machine-gunned along with other Muslims in front of the veterinarian's wife and daughter.

The man said that he had counted at least fifty bodies of Muslims in the gardens of homes back from Zvornik's main street, where four story homes with steep Alpine roofs crowded against the towering escarpment of Vratolo-mac, the "neck-breaking hill" that overlooks the town.

The man said that one of the dead was a 17-year-old Serbian girl whose throat had been cut.

"She was slaughtered just because she asked them not to do anything to the Muslims," he said.

—International Herald Tribune
Saturday–Sunday, May 23–24, 1992

2

REBELLION
AGAINST CREATION

The feminist critique of Niebuhr, developed by Valerie Saiving, Judith Plaskow, and Susan Nelson respectively,[1] provides my entry into the task of showing that within the example of Niebuhr's sustained development of sin as a rebellion against God, one can find the means to reverse the concept. My argument proceeds from Niebuhr's need to absorb the sin related to nature into the sin of the spirit so that he might find for both the required limitations in the infinity of God. The feminist redevelopment of sin in relation to nature (sensuousness for Niebuhr, hiding for Nelson) effectively establishes the sin of nature in its own right, no longer absorbed into the sin of the spirit. This in turn suggests 1) the ability to account for the human capacity for infinity from within creation, 2) a redefinition of self-transcendence that takes account of the social nature of self-transcendence, and 3) an accountability of the human spirit within creation, so that 4) violation of this accountability is more aptly described as a "rebellion against creation" than "rebellion against God."

The feminist scholars variously point out that Niebuhr failed to develop the full implications of his insight into the sin of sensuousness, and instead absorbed it into the sin of pride. Indeed, they suggest that by doing so, Niebuhr himself may have fallen into the

---

[1] Valerie Saiving Goldstein, "The Human Situation: A Feminine View," *Journal of Religion* 40 (April 1960): 100–112; Judith Plaskow, *Sex, Sin and Grace: Women's Experience and the Theologies of Reinhold Niebuhr and Paul Tillich* (New York: University Press of America, 1980). Susan Nelson Dunfee, "The Sin of Hiding," *Soundings* LXV/3 (Fall 1982): 316–327.

sin of pride, since it is the nature of pride to absolutize oneself, ignoring the claims of others. But the sin of sensuousness needs to be developed in its own right.

Niebuhr described sensuousness through nature as the excessive gratification of the human appetites, and through spirit as the flight from freedom into an immersion in nature. In both cases, one seeks deification of either the self or another, by which Niebuhr meant that one seeks one's limits and one's security either through the self or through the other, rather than through trust in God. The feminist critique by Saiving, Plaskow, and Nelson does not challenge Niebuhr on this point. Rather, each feminist supplements Niebuhr's description of sin by giving a fuller development of his brief treatment of the sin of sensuousness.[2] The feminist scholars see the sin of pride as describing the sins of the powerful who refuse to recognize the rightful boundaries of others, and the sin of hiding as the refusal of the responsibility to become a self that is so often the plight of women and men who are not in positions of power. In the process, they effectively show that Niebuhr's one-sided treatment of sin through the notion of pride demonstrates the bias of his culture and gender, and therefore the particularity rather than universality of his description of sin.

Uniformly absent in the critique of each woman is any description of the sin of sensuousness/hiding as being a search for a substitute for God. Niebuhr, writing from the perspective of the powerful, sees all sin as a striving to be God or to replace God. The feminists, writing from the perspective of the marginalized, find the problem of sin rooted in the great challenge of becoming oneself. Their point of reference is not a command of God which one defiantly violates, but the demeaning demands of social custom which one feels powerless to violate. The frequent equation drawn by persons in authority between rebellion against God and rebellion against any authority, particularly their own, increases the problem. For the oppressed, the problem is not defining limits, but defying limits. Those given to the sin of pride increase the problems of those given to the sin of sensuousness. When sensuousness is absorbed into pride, the violation is simply repeated at the level of theory. The sin of sensuousness only emerges in its seriousness when it is separated from the sin of pride.

---

[2] Plaskow and Nelson in particular use their redevelopment of the sin of sensuousness as grounds for rejection of the ideal of self-sacrificial love. They point out that while

But if the sin of sensuousness is not absorbed into pride, then certain things follow for naming all sin as rebellion against God. Niebuhr's absorption of sensuousness into pride is not simply an oversight in his system, but in fact is necessary in order to maintain the primacy of rebellion against God as the fundamental nature of sin. He argues that since the human transcends nature, only that which also transcends nature in an even greater capacity can provide humanity with its limits, norms, judgment, and meaning. He finds this greater transcendence in God—more specifically, in the will of God. But the limits and meaning that the human requires relate to the whole of a person, nature and spirit. There is thus a hierarchical sense in which nature, while important in its own right, must not simply qualify spirit, but must be absorbed into spirit in order to come under the norm provided by the transcendent will of God. Nature as well as spirit finds its required limits in the will of God. Therefore, to defy the limits imposed upon our natural appetites or refuse to exercise our freedom to become a self even in the realm of nature is to sin against norms that are mediated by spirit, and derived from the ultimately transcendent Spirit, God. In this sense, the sin of sensuousness must be absorbed into the sin of pride in order to receive its norms and be judged by its norms as mediated through spirit.

The feminist critique, by extricating nature from its absorption in spirit, suggests to me that nature in its own right should be examined for the source of transcendence that Niebuhr thought could only be found in spirit. That is, his systematic reason for absorbing nature into spirit was the principle that there is no sufficient form of transcendence in nature whereby limits or norms for humanity can be found. But is this in fact the case? Plaskow points to nature as providing a form of transcendence beyond the arbitrary norms of society: "Nature operates within and around us in ways that give content to our lives, and we may experience a sense of continuity with nature for which our involvement in its vitalities and forms is not an adequate illustration."[3] If one can see that the plight of the sin of hiding finds some alleviation in nature in a way that includes an element of transcendence (" . . . for which our involvement in its vitalities and forms is not an adequate illustra-

---

self-sacrificial love may well correct the masculine sin of pride, it actually exacerbates woman's sin of hiding from her own freedom.
[3] Plaskow, *Sex, Sin, and Grace.*, p. 73

tion"), might one not explore the modes of transcendence provided through nature to see what limitations nature might provide for the human mode of transcendence?

Transcendence in nature is relative; it is the conditioning transcendence of finitude. In its most obvious sense, each entity in nature transcends all others simply through the uniqueness of its own identity, which can be reduced to no other. But this mode of transcendence is gained not through isolation from all others, but through relation to all others. What an entity is depends upon where it is, when it is, and how it responds to the various influences upon it, whether those influences be primarily the atoms and molecules that are the building blocks of the visible and invisible universe, or whether those influences are the social influences of culture and family. Such a mode of transcendence is extraordinarily ordinary, qualifying every existent reality. It does not provide the vantage point of a lofty perspective surveying the universe from above. It does provide, through the very thoroughness of its relationality, a vantage point that transcends the rest of the world through its uniqueness, even while it relates to the rest of the world through its relativity. It may indeed survey the universe from within.

Niebuhr saw transcendence as relating to infinity, but as he also saw in relationship to time, finitude is no stranger to infinity. One need not go to a realm completely beyond finitude in order to find infinity. The transcendent infinity envisioned by Niebuhr was a boundless infinity without number; the still transcendent infinity encountered within finitude is a boundless infinity *with* number. The stars, in principle, are numerable; the sands of the sea, in principle, are numerable; but are they in fact numerable? Is it not the case that the infinity of numbers is matched by the infinite ongoingness of creation itself? Creation is marked by both transience and permanence: one star dies, but another is born; one grain of sand is finally ground until it is no longer sand, but another tumbles into the sea from the river. Contemporary chaos theory speaks of fractals that are finite patterns creating literally infinite variations, but a similar illustration much closer to home is the human face itself. The one invariable structure of eyes, nose, cheeks, mouth is inexhaustibly infinite in its uniqueness of forms, such that even in the case of identical twins there is distinguishable variation. Finitude is not the opposite of infinity, but is through its very transience a form of infinity. In this sense, one is reminded of Plato's insight that time is the moving image of eternity. But of course one might also say that infinity is a form of finitude, and our concepts of eternity but the stilled image of time. Finitude *is* finitude through its infinite variations of forms. Infinity then is not the opposite of either finitude or nature, but an aspect of both.

The objector, of course, would claim that since the infinity of finitude is in and through its very transience, that it is not a true infinity at all: in principle, there may have been a time when there was nothing and there may be a time when there will again be nothing—although the word "time" in such a case is a misnomer. But since the infinity of finitude is concrete and not abstract, the possibility of the cessation of finite reality as a whole is not to be equated with an actual cessation. It is just as possible to say that while various forms of existence do indeed begin and end, existence per se is infinite. We have no way of knowing that it is not, and therefore we must work with what we do know: infinity is a form of finitude, and finitude is a form of infinity.

If infinity and finitude are dyadic in nature, then it may be that God is also included in such a dyadic construction. One could posit that the difference between infinity as attributed to God and infinity as attributed to nature is that God may well be infinitely one, whereas creation is infinitely many. Even here, however, one cannot make absolute distinctions, for God contains manyness within an essential unity, and the world certainly knows the unity of each finite form that constitutes it as many. But in either case, finitude and infinity can no longer be viewed as ultimate opposites; they are as dyadically entwined as Niebuhr began to indicate through his insightful analysis of humanity as nature and spirit.

What, then, of transcendence? If infinity permeates nature, then the human capacity for the infinite does not place us outside of nature, but very much at home within nature. Our own capacity for transcendence, whether of self or of the world, is not a solitary thing, but in fact is woven in and through other modes of transcendence in a way that is at once finite and infinite. It is finite in that it is concretely related to concrete others, and it is infinite in that through these relationships, we are always confronted with possibilities that stretch into infinity.

Niebuhr defined self-transcendence vertically, with a reach toward infinity at great heights above nature. This allowed him to make the transcendent God the criterion of sin. But if infinity is no stranger to nature, then one can develop a "horizontal" notion of self-transcendence, such that it is gained through a certain "withness in" the world, not an "over and above" the world. In this case, the world itself is capable of providing the criterion of sin.

Self-transcendence can be established through the social and temporal construction of the self in at least three modes: in relation to one's own past through memory; in relation to others in the present through empathy, and in relation to the future through imagination. In all three cases, the ground of transcendence is not the ultimate transcendence of deity, but the mundane transcendence of a world that is in itself finite *and* infinite.

The further importance of defining the forms of transcendence is that the human act of violating well-being always involves a failure of one or more of the modes of transcendence. One can roughly correlate a failure of transcendence through memory with the perpetuation of the past as violence; the failure of empathy has a correlation with violation mediated through the solidarity of the human race; and the failure of imagination relates to violence perpetuated through social structures. But of course if a failure of transcendence is involved in sin, then the very capacity for transcendence becomes a resource for dealing with these modes of sin. For these reasons I must extend this argument against Niebuhr concerning the creaturely versus godly ground of transcendence, and spell out in some detail the nature of human transcendence as memory, empathy, and imagination.

Memory is fundamental, since it is presupposed by the second and third forms of transcendence. That is, to relate empathically to others presupposes a self who relates, and this self is established through memory. Furthermore, empathy toward others relies heavily on memories of empathy received from others, so that a sense of one's own selfhood is basic to empathy for another's selfhood. With regard to imagination, that too presupposes memory. Imagination envisions a different future, but difference itself requires difference *from*. Memory of the past and cognizance of the present are presupposed in the act of imagining a future that transcends the present. All three modes of self-transcendence—memory, empathy, and imagination—provide a transcendence within nature for the continuous defining of human nature.

With regard to the basic form of self-transcendence, or memory, there are two forms to be considered. The first deals with one's relation to the immediate past, and the other considers one's sense of the self as historical, relating to the fullness of one's whole past.

Both constitute transcendence of the immediately present self through memory.

Memory as consciousness of the immediate past is the process of lifting some of the myriad relations that affect us into awareness. Like all of nature, we exist within networks of complex interrelationships that deeply affect our becoming selves. The phenomenon of self-consciousness is our ability to reflect upon our experience. We lift some relationships (though never all, since consciousness is a selective function) to prominence through contrasting them with others. Simple consciousness would be immersion in the awareness of relation without regard to the temporality of relation. Self-consciousness, however, derives from and attends to the successive states of consciousness, almost as if one were observing them. Rather than being immersed in the present alone, one perceives the present in and through one's memory of the immediate or distant past. Thus self-consciousness is always a mediated consciousness that transcends itself through relation to itself. It knows that it knows.

Given this continuous emergence of the self in the presence of self-consciousness, it is but a simple step to note self-consciousness not simply in terms of the immediate past, but in terms of one's full past. On the one hand, the self is neither the past which is transcended alone, nor the immediately transcending element alone, but the temporal event that is both. That is, the transcendent self *emerges* from its own past in response to that past. The emergent self is therefore a historical self, a self already molded by the very past it transcends. But insofar as this is a continuous process, the temporal nature of the self produces successive layers, like the ever growing sedimentation in a river bed. Memory encompasses not simply the immediate past, but the compilation of many past moments. The self is constituted as historical.

This historicity sets down parameters to which the transcendent self must perforce attend; it cannot do otherwise. Hence self-transcendence is always conditioned by the very past that it transcends. The self is a historically constructed self, created through the successiveness of its continually emerging transcendence.

But it *transcends* this determining past, which means that the continuance of the self involves the possibility of changing—or reinforcing—perspectives on its own past. The transcending self must reconfigure the past anew in light of the new influences brought to bear upon the self by its wider environment. These new elements offer changing perspectives on the meaning of one's past. Thus one is conditioned by the past, but not limited by the past. Therefore, one can transcend the past.

The past can be broadened because of the selective function of consciousness. Consciousness is itself the narrowing of focus, the creation of a foreground and a background by lifting "this" rather than "that" into significance.

In any one moment, far more impinges upon the self than can be cognated. Even less can be carried over into the continuing self in the form of significant memory. For example, an adult remembers childhood not in its detail, but in terms of an overall retention of feeling that may be positive or negative in tone, with some of the occasions that contributed to that type of feeling available for remembrance at any time. But by far most of the events of childhood are no longer immediately accessible to memory. The remembered past of childhood is like the experience of crossing a brook on stepping stones—the stones upon which one steps may be the only ones seen, but they are there because of the whole rocky bottom of the brook. There are many stones, hidden from the surface, and their presence supports the stones upon which one steps. One remembers a few events from childhood, but there were many, many more that are no longer easily available to conscious memory.

When those stepping stones of memory are severe or traumatic in nature, it can be as if they were not stepping stones at all, but a solid ledge allowing no other facts, neither the other stones nor the flow of water continually molding them. There is only the ledge, and such memories can cause great pain in the present. But in fact there was not only the ledge. There were other events, which if allowed into memory can recontextualize those stones of trauma. One has a wider past than that which is immediately remembered. One can transcend the "ledgelike" character of present memory by recovering the fuller past, and thus offering a different configuration for its meaning.

The same is true when one has blotted out the traumatic memory, conceptualizing the past as having been only the sunshine glancing off the surface of the brook. There is shallowness in not recognizing the fullness of the rocks beneath. Recognized or not, those rocks deeply affect the present. To gain a wider memory of the past is to transcend any one pattern presently conditioning one from that past. Thus the self-transcendence over one's past is gained not only in spite of the conditioning of that past, but sometimes even through that conditioning.

The sense of infinity that so intrigued Niebuhr in self-transcendence can easily be deduced from the fullness of relation through which the self is formed. The self is formed in creative responsiveness to the influences received from the whole world, and as we have seen, finitude is a form of infinity. But while the self emerges in response to these influences, it is impossible ever to bring them all to awareness. There is always that which eludes us: we are not "self-contained." We are essentially each an open self, embedded within a world touched by infinity. Neither the totality of our own selfhood nor, even less so, the totality of the other can ever be apprehended by the necessarily selective function of consciousness. Thus there is a "more than" to consciousness that is always intuited, but never grasped. We sense the infinity in which we participate.

In no instance can there be an isolated, solipsistic consciousness. The personal is social. While it is indeed one's immediate past self to which one relates, that self is constituted in and through relation to all others influencing its universe—as, indeed, is the present, apprehending self, whose being, including its consciousness, will be offered to the next moment. Self-consciousness is an open reality, formed through a deep responsiveness to energies received from others, particularly the "otherness" of its own past. Hence this first mode of transcendence for the self, or relating knowingly to one's own past, is the basis for the second mode of self-transcendence, which is empathy.

To relate to one's immediately past self is to relate to the relations within that past. The second mode of self-transcendence, or empathy, can—but need not—emerge from this internalization of relationships. The first mode of self-transcendence is fundamental because it is necessary; it is entailed in the very constitution of self-consciousness. But the second mode, empathy, relates to the *how* of one's response, and this is variable. Since we in one sense internalize the other through relation, it is within the realm of possibility to relate to the other as no more than an extension of the self. Such simple awareness of others does not constitute this second form of self-transcendence, for if we respond to others without regard to their "otherness," as if we had absorbed the other totally into the self, we have not transcended the self. Rather, we have absolutized the self, as if the self were a solitary individual. This, of course, would be analogous to Niebuhr's sin of pride, but whereas Niebuhr defined pride as utilizing one's self-transcendence to overstep one's set limits, this understanding of pride is a failure to utilize self-transcendence at all. It is first a failure of self-transcendence, and second, a failure to act in accordance with the reality of relation.

A contrary mode of relating to the other that also fails to become empathic self-transcendence is not to make the self absolute, but to make the other absolute, or what the feminists point to as the sin of hiding. One can so identify with the other that one effectively loses—or never develops—a sense of self. In this case, there is no self-transcendence, for the presupposition of self-transcendence is in fact the presence of a self. To lose the self through absorbing the perspective of the other is doubly to lose, for on the one hand the aspect of infinity that pervades all finite selves means one can never completely identify with the other, since the fullness of the other is elusive. To pretend to do so is to absolutize an objectified other, which means one loses sight of the real other. And on the other hand, one has also lost the rightful sense of self as the centered self who enters into relation. Whereas for Niebuhr the sin of sensuousness (or hiding) resulted from a refusal of one's freedom (and therefore a refusal of one's self-transcending possibilities), in this understanding the absolutization of the other is in fact the overreaching of self-transcendence to the point of losing the self. It is a mode of transcendence ungrounded in the self.

Self-transcendence through empathy emerges when one relates to the other as the related other who is also subject. Such self-transcendence is the enrichment of the self as well as an enrichment of the other. By bringing the relationship itself into view, both self and other are at the same time preserved and transformed. The preservation is due to the fact that relationship requires more than one in differentiation. If either self or other is absolutized, then the differentiation is blurred, and the relation as relation ceases to be significant. But empathy retains an appreciative differentiation between self and other that honors the subjectivity of each. Hence there is a preservation rather than absorption of otherness.

The transformation is through the mutuality that empathy creates. One brings another's experience into one's own, albeit with the natural limitation of perspective that finitude entails, and offers one's own experience to another. This provides an intuited enlargement of perspective that can deepen or challenge one's attitudes and actions. To open oneself to the legitimacy of the other's point of view through empathy is to open oneself to transformation and spiritual growth. In the ongoingness of relation, this contributes to the inexhaustibility of the relationship, for insofar as each is open to the other, there is a dynamism that continuously creates new dimensions in the relationship. The empathic relationship is always transcending itself as its subjects participate in the infinite variations that are possible even with the one relation—like fractals that are always the same, yet never the same. Self-transcendence through empathy, then, entails a regard for the other as other, openness to the other as subject, and transformation of the self.

In the third mode of self-transcendence, one imagines a future that does not yet exist. Since it does not exist, to imagine it by definition means to transcend the present self. Just as transcendence through empathy drew upon infinity within relation, transcendence through imagination draws upon infinite possibilities. Imagination is itself the impinging of infinity upon finitude, confronting or even creating the finite consciousness through its call to active participation in many ways of being. Through imagination, one transcends one's present circumstances and envisions a future, whether that future relates to an education, a profession, persons, or wider conditions in the world. Imagination transcends the present self through its vision of a different state of affairs. Through this vision of the future, the self participates in the transformation of the present. As the poet Rilke said, "The future enters into us, in order to transform itself in us long before it happens."

As noted, the three modes of self-transcendence each emphasize a different modality of time. Transcendence through self-consciousness as memory evolves through one's relation to one's past, and the creation of one's historicity. Transcendence through empathy is a present phenomenon created through relation to the other as subjective other. And transcendence through imagination calls upon the novelty of that which may yet be, the future. But while each mode emphasizes a different modality of time, they are by no means mutually exclusive. To the contrary: without the first, neither of the other two would be possible. And both the second and third can evoke different remembrances from one's past.

Empathy and imagination can richly condition one another. Empathy without imagination can lead to an imprisoning of a relationship within its past or present manifestations; imagination without empathy can lead to a violation of self-transcendence through a failure to account for one's social relatedness. Thus both empathy and imagination are possible as distinctive modes, but they function most fully in relation to each other.

Niebuhr's understanding of self-transcendence as being rooted in the infinity of God created a "vertical" understanding of the self as spirit, and led to a notion of sin as primarily against God. An understanding of self-transcendence located in the infinity within nature creates a "horizontal" understanding of the self, and therefore leads to a notion of sin defined in and through the limitations suggested by that horizon.

One is a self among others, with others, and this "withness" conditions one's own becoming. The self-transcendence of one is met by the self-transcendence of countless others, each of which provides both a limitation and an invitation. One need not be a Hobbesian to recognize that society exists in part through the need to order competing and common interests among people, thus setting limits, which may or may not be just. But limitation is only part of the result of a world of mutually conditioning self-transcendent persons. More important, the ontological interdependence of many is already an invitation to a social order that transcends mere regulation of competing interests. It is an invitation to the mutual enrichment of one another through communities of personal relationships. Thus finitude in its very multiplicity of self-transcendent subjects provides open limits and possibilities for infinite variety in the ways of being together.

But humanity is not simply interdependent within its own sphere, it is interdependent within the wider world of nature. A self-transcendence developed vertically places humans above nature; a self-transcendence developed horizontally emphasizes the human continuity with nature. We are of the earth, earthly, experiencing our interdependence through our fragility as well as through our capacity to transform nature into a world. Preservation of human existence requires a preservation of the environment upon which we depend. A wider issue is the value of the environment in and for itself, independently of human concerns, which will enter the discussion more directly in chapter four. For the present purpose of finding boundaries for creaturely conduct within nature itself, one can say that boundaries are plentifully given. The interdependence of creaturely existence itself suggests boundaries defining mutual well-being.

Human existence, then, is related to a potentially infinite host of others. Through self-transcendence as memory one can lift relationships into awareness; through empathic self-transcendence, one can become an expansive self involved in mutual enrichment with others; through imaginative self-transcendence, one can actively participate in the ever-new and open creation of a future. In all three modes, the self inescapably has to do with others, just as others inescapably have to do with oneself. Each person is a self in and through relation.

When, then, one responds to relation by violating the well-being of another, one has lessened the richness of experience not only for the other, but also for all (including the self) who exist interdependently with that other. Given the openness of interdependent existence, it is impossible to violate one without having an effect upon all. Thus any single violation has communal effects. The same is true with regard to one's relation to the world of nature: To violate any aspect of the well-being of nature is to violate the well-being of all, including the self, who are interdependent with that aspect of nature. Every violation has individual and social effects. If one can presuppose that well-being is better than ill-being, then we can say that every violation is a rebellion against the well-being of creation.

Developing a horizontal, or world-related, interpretation of human self-transcendence allows us to bring the social nature of the self into view, and through that social nature, to account for the vulnerability that allows us both richness and destructiveness of being. It brings creaturely interdependence and therefore creaturely obligation into view. The unnecessary violation of this interdependence and obligation is a direct sin against the well-being of creation. Sin, then, is rebellion against creation.

I began this chapter by stating that the feminist critique of Niebuhr's theology provided the means to extend the feminist analysis so that it doesn't simply supplement Niebuhr, but overturns him. Saiving, Plaskow, and Nelson respectively argued that what Niebuhr called the sins of nature actually related strongly to that which is problematic in the existence of women and those who are marginalized in society, while the sins of pride more usually apply to men and those in power. But to critique Niebuhr thus is implicitly to accept the dichotomous identification of women with nature and men with spirit that has for so long stereotyped women. Nor does the critique deal with the metaphysical reasons that prompted Niebuhr to absorb nature into spirit. Niebuhr was convinced that human transcendence over self and nature could only be explained

by a non-mystical participation in an infinite Spirit that also transcends all selves and nature, God. Since human existence is thus
rooted in divine existence, the norms and limitations for human
existence are ultimately grounded in the will of God. By absorbing
nature into spirit, nature, too, became subject to the norms of spirit
derived from the will of God.

While I have challenged these aspects of Niebuhr's thought, I
have not challenged his assumption that infinity is involved in defining human nature, nor his assumption that this "more than" to
human existence is the basis upon which one builds an understanding of sin. Instead, I have argued that the "more than" defining
human existence is derived from the infinity that is woven in and
through all finite existence. This means that the norms for developing one's humanity can be found within the structures of interrelatedness that make for communal well-being. Within these
structures, the development of one's humanity takes place through
the three modes of self-transcendence. The pride and sensuousness
defined by Niebuhr are absorbed in my development not into a
dichotomy of nature and spirit, but into distortions of the second
mode of transcendence, empathy. The insights of Plaskow and Nelson concerning the predominance of Niebuhrian pride among men
and the powerful, and of sensuousness among women and the marginalized, still hold. But there is no longer any need to identify
pride and sensuousness with spirit and nature respectively. Rather,
both follow from failures of empathy, with men and women alike
quite capable of these failures. Cultural conditions and personal
sensitivities account for the differences, rather than a primary identification with either spirit or nature.

I also began this chapter with an eye-witness account of the Serbian slaughter of Muslims in a Bosnian town. The witness specifically mentioned a veterinarian and a seventeen-year old Serbian
girl who had pleaded with the soldiers to spare the Muslims. While
the location in this particular case is what was once Yugoslavia, and
the assailants are Serbian, the crime is like those that have been
committed by ethnic groups and nationalities the world over. With
but few changes, it could have been an account of United States
activity against indigenous Americans, or the Pol Pot repression of
Cambodians, or Nazi persecution of Jews and Gypsies, or Azer-
baijans against the Armenians. Alternatively, it might have been
adapted to describe the actions of one indigenous American group
against another, or of Cambodian conduct, or Jews, or Gypsies, or

Armenians: there are no ethnicities or nations that can plead innocent to such conduct against those it perceives to be outsiders.

To name all such actions as sin is to assert 1) these actions should not have happened, 2) there is human responsibility for these actions, and 3) there is an alternative vision for how interdependent human beings can resolve disputes. The victims of sin in the given news report are multiple: most conspicuously, the veterinarian, the other 50 dead Muslims, and the seventeen year old girl. Their murderers cut off their lives, robbing them of their future. The sins are most directly against these dead, for their "well-being" has been violated in a manner incapable of historical redress.

The second round of victims includes the veterinarian's wife and daughter, and the sixty-year-old man telling the story; implied as well are families and friends of all those who were killed. They too experience death, albeit for them, the death of a relationship. The continuing effects of the sin will be as various as the circumstances of those injured, and will range from the psychic scars of children to the inevitable poverty of new widows and their children.

The townspeople themselves also suffer from this sin. They experience the deep mourning of grief especially for the loss of these lives, but also for the loss of the town they once knew. Such enormous violation of the town robs it of its former measure of security not only in the present, but throughout the lifetimes of those who live through the atrocities.

Also sinned against are the local and global Muslim community, and likewise the Christian community insofar as the merging of religious and nationalist feelings contributed to the vicious persecution of the Muslims by the Christians. The well-being of these communities has been violated, the Muslims by the pain of loss, and the Christians by the shame of participation in inflicting that loss.

The final victims to be named, simply from the account given in the article, are the murderers themselves. The perpetrators of this sin, in sinning against these others, have also sinned against themselves by brutalizing their own humanity. Sin is a spiral, with the deepest evil inflicted against the murdered, who are cut off from the forms of redeeming transformation that are still possible for others within the continuing history of human life. But this central violation spins off others, touching and destroying in increasing circles, finally lessening the well-being of all, including the perpetrators. Sin is not a contained act, but an extended event in an interdependent world.

With regard to those who committed this sin of state-endorsed murder, we can apply the theories developed in this chapter in a negative way. That is, thus far we can only show that relative to the murderers, the sin was a failure of self-transcendence. The issue is not that they transcended themselves too far by appropriating a deistic role, but that they refused to engage in the forms of self-transcendence essential to their humanity. The failure of memory is that they have locked themselves into a past of endless circles of vengeance, denying the wider memory of the richness of diverse traditions. The failure of empathy is most apparent in their response to the girl who pleaded mercy for others and in their actual slaughter of the Muslims. The failure of imagination is the apparent inability to seek a future that goes beyond the perpetuation of their own kind and their own power.

But more than failure of transcendence occurred. The account shows a savage power that scorns any form of transcendence. For Niebuhr, the root of this power was the fundamental insecurity arising from anxiety concerning one's existence—an insecurity to which one ought to respond by trusting in God. Instead of trusting God, one tries to be God, and this is the "whence" of the murder of this seventeen year old girl and the others. It is the result of one's own idolatry, the primal sin of rebellion against God. But to understand sin as rebellion against creation requires a redefinition of the power of sin sufficient to the savagery in the news account; this topic will be explored in chapter five. For the present, however, I submit that the sin described in the news report is a direct violation of the well-being of creation, and as such is a rebellion against creation. Because of this, it is also, derivatively, a rebellion against God. And to this topic I must now turn.

SIN

Simon Mthimkulu died after police arrested him in Sebo-keng Township on July 14th. A friend arrested with Mthimkulu, himself beaten and then released, later stated that he saw officers viciously kick and beat Simon and drop a "huge rock" on his rib cage. Police had told Simon's mother that they had released the youth. However, two days later, she found her son's body at a mortuary. His face was caked in blood.

—*Amnesty Action*
Winter, 1993

SIN AGAINST GOD

S in as the unnecessary violation of the well-being of any aspect of creation is my primary definition of sin. The language of sin as a "rebellion against creation" indicates not a primacy of one being against another, but a primacy of the well-being of all, against which one rebels in sin. In this sense, sin can be called a "rebellion against creation." While the focus is on the violation of creation, in a relational universe the violation of creation is *also* a violation of God. If God feels the effects of every sin, then every sin is not only against creation, it is against God as well. Therefore, sin as rebellion against creation necessarily entails sin against God.

The grounds for making this assertion depend upon the following steps: 1) the presupposition of God in Christian thought; 2) a relational understanding of creation and God;[1] 3) God's experience of the world and therefore God's suffering with the world, so that 4) all sin is also sin against God.

Christian faith is essentially theistic, maintaining that Jesus Christ

---

[1] I have intentionally moved to the phrase, "relational theology" rather than the usual term, "process theology." All theologies based upon the work of Alfred North Whitehead deal with relationships as central to existence, and the phrase "relational theology" communicates this. "Process" denotes the dynamism of existence, and assuredly implies this relational essence. Insofar as this implication is not always obvious to those unfamiliar with Whitehead's works, I have chosen to use "relational theology" as the more explicitly descriptive term.

While this entire volume is an exploration based upon relational theology, this chapter more than the others requires some explication of Whitehead's system. Hence the middle portions of this chapter recapitulate the philosophical system in order to show why sin against creation is also sin against God.

reveals something of who God is, and that God relates to us. It takes no great knowledge of Christian history to realize that such a fundamental statement is capable of a great many differing interpretations and elaborations, but the conviction that God is in Christ and that God wills our good threads its way through all of these.

Christian faith is theistic not because it *proves* the existence and character of God, but because it *presumes* the existence and character of God. The attempts within Christian thought to prove the existence and character of God already presuppose that which they seek to prove, and thus serve more as expressions of faith than as proofs of faith. As such, theologians work out the reasonableness of faith within a particular construal of reality that is already shaped by Christian faith. In the process, they strengthen, expand, and to some extent transform that construal of reality, creating the Christian tradition. The perduring supposition is that in and through Jesus Christ, we have to do not simply with human history, but with God.

The challenges to this presupposition are many, with the strongest coming from the recognition of the way all thought is conditioned by its context. If former ages could confidently expound on the nature of God, as if sure knowledge applicable to all times and places had been obtained independently of cultural context, such absolutist claims are no longer tenable. Human thinking, whether about God or nature or about its own self, emerges from an ever-flowing confluence of events, converging, separating, reconfiguring, much like the eddies of a rushing river. We think from the midst of experience, no matter what our capacities for self-transcendence, and not from some privileged position that allows us to survey all of existence unmuddied by our perspective. Our thinking reflects our interactive experiences and our generalizations from those experiences. Our social and personal histories, and the hopes and prejudices attendant upon them, enter into our generalizations, thus belying any pretensions to disinterested observation or universal truth.

Our thinking reflects the great flux of existence as we experience it, but it also reflects continuities. There are the agreed upon commonalities. We are *we*: social beings, living in interaction with others like us. We are embodied creatures, with a distinctive human anatomy that endows us with certain restraints. We require food, air, water, and a certain degree of temperature in order to live. We are mortal in that we die, and our lifespan gives us more or less endurance than the continuities of things around us. We depend upon these other endurances, such as the givenness of the solar system and its own sustenance of the planet of which we are a part. Such commonalities undergird all human experience, and we have developed sciences to investigate the various natures of all these things that we construe into a world. But even here, our thinking about such things is interpretive, perspectival, and therefore must be framed with an openness to change. Whether in the various scientific/humanistic disciplines or in personal thinking, our understanding about the commonalities of human existence is woven throughout with interpretations concerning the significance of these commonalities, and as will be discussed subsequently, these interpretations have enormous social repercussions. We investigate, reflect, project, and proclaim ever from the midst of things.

But this thinking from the midst of things is no reason to cease thinking, or on principle to disavow our discoveries or our generalizations. It is only to say that thought should not be plucked from its context, like flowers cut off from their life's energies and preserved for so brief a time in our vases. Our investment in our own generalizations must be explicit, so that our finely wrought theories are made ever open to reconsideration, revision, or rejection. Continual openness to the flux and continuities of things, to divergent ways of generalizing from the ambiguities of experience, and to the limited and conditioned nature of all thought provides the context in which we nonetheless dare to think and to generalize and to offer our thought to wider communities for critique and response. There can be no presumption of finality to the task of thinking that admittedly takes place from the midst of things.

But neither is there a presumption of futility to such a task. To the contrary, the "perspectival ontologies" we develop will be the richer for their acknowledgment of the peculiarities and particularities of their grounding. There is a paradoxical sense in which "truth" is only attained through such perspectival ontologies. To claim absolute validity to thought, when in fact thought can only be perspectival, is to falsify that which one claims to know. But to recognize the particularist nature of thought is to recognize the relational nature of knowledge, and the sense in which that which is known inescapably includes the knower. Knowledge is an event rather than a fact. When the knower abstracts him or herself from this event, then the "known" is falsified.

Insofar as the knower is a social being, existing in and through many circles of relationships, then the event of knowledge cannot be confined to a single individual. The language through which one knows is socially derived, and concretely related to the common continuities of human experience. Thus one's knowledge, though individually experienced, is socially grounded and therefore communicable. And while one's own circle of relationships is most apt to participate meaningfully in that which one knows, given the common human experience of flux and continuity within the context of our planet, knowledge from one community of discourse is to some degree communicable to other communities of discourse. A degree of commonality of human experience is the basis, and the self-transcendence of empathy and imagination is the means. Thus the event of knowledge that transpires between a subject and an object or between subjects is at once perspectival, social, and communicable. But it is not absolute.

So then, Christian thought takes place from the midst of flux and continuity that is ever shaped into a world of meaning. It shares with all peoples the experience of the world as both flux and continuity, but its particular shaping of this experience is deeply influenced by the presupposition that even in the midst of history we can know God. This presupposition undergirds Christian experience and is naturally reinforced by Christian experience. One does not go "under" the experience to prove that it is so, and in this sense knowledge of God and faith in God are inseparable terms.

To base one's faith in God on the conviction that the character of God is revealed in Jesus Christ is already to say that what we can know of God is necessarily mediated through history. But if it is mediated through history, then what is called revelation shares in the ambiguities of history and must perforce be a limited and particular form of knowledge. This is multiply so: on the one hand, if God is revealed in Jesus Christ, then God is revealed within particular circumstances relating to a Judean culture that was deeply influenced by the Greek and Roman cultures of its time. But if God is revealed to *us* through that remote history, then our perceptions of that revelation are themselves conditioned by our own time and place. Yet again, if God is revealed to *us as Christians* through that foundational history, then we read that history not only through the lens of our own personal and cultural spectacles, but also through the multiple lenses provided for us through the successive interpretations of the gospel throughout Christian history. Thus the revelation of God given in Jesus Christ is of all things incarnational and therefore historical, mediated through particularity not once, but again and again. The knowledge of God in Christ, then, is a variable rather than single event; thus no single interpretation of Christ can claim to be final knowledge of God, or even a final knowledge of what God has done for us in Christ.

But finality is not necessary in order to constitute the event of faith as knowledge. The knowledge of God that grows from the midst of things must confess that what we know of God is that which relates to us. But this, of course, is the salvific component of knowledge of God: It is a knowledge for *us*, in an event that includes *us*. Far from being the underminer of faith, perspectival knowledge has been the undergirding of faith throughout Christian history. Through faith, we say that God adapts to our condition, not only through an incarnation in Jesus, but also in all God's dealings with us. God meets us from, in, and through the midst of things.

This God who is thus accessible to faith may indeed exist independently of the universe, or may not. Reason working through faith certainly speculates on such a question. But the speculation itself begins from the historical process, which is the place of meeting and thus provides the stuff for revelation. Our speculations beyond that which is given for our sustenance in history move into realms of possibility and probability. Such speculations are grounded in faith, but cannot provide the grounds for faith. Christian faith finds its ground in God's incarnational involvement in the world, an involvement which participates, as well it ought, in the ambiguities of cultural relativity.

Naturally the center of this revelation, Jesus Christ as mediated through Christian texts, has generated almost as many interpretations as there have been interpreters. Albert Schweitzer's wry remark that the lives of Jesus produced in 19th century scholarship are so many portraits of the idealized hopes of the scholars may well be expanded to cover all of our Jesusologies and Christologies, and so it should be. Were it not so, the God we say we see in the gospel would be a remote God, perceivable at a distance but not directly accessible to us. That we see God not only through the guise of the gospel, but also through the particularities of our own time and place, is essential to a faith that claims to be based upon an incarnation, or a God who is with us.

Whereas the traditional mode of thinking about Christian faith tended to de-historicize the contents of faith as if in fact it were possible to have a perception of God untouched by the ambiguities of history, theological thinking from the midst of things must put away such pretensions, and embrace fully the incarnational nature not only of Christ, but of Christian faith itself. "Now we see through a glass, darkly," wrote the Apostle, and that "now" must be extended to cover every tenet of Christian faith. We know God in and through the ambiguities of our personal and cultural histories. Thus we know God relatively, not absolutely. Our knowledge will be pertinent to those who participate to some extent in our perspective, or who desire to learn more about our perspective; knowledge that is an event is communicable. But it ought not dress itself up for a masquerade ball, parading as universal truth. It is perspectival truth: knowledge as an event.

But it is perspectival *knowledge*. God has acted for us in Christ. Where else and how else God may be acting, whether on some other part of our own planet or in the outermost galaxies, is certainly material for our speculation, but it is not given to us as knowledge. What we do know is that God has acted and does act for us in Jesus Christ, that this reality we name God undergirds and supports us, judges and redeems us, and calls us to wider circles of caring for the well-being of creation. Our faith comes in part from our encounter with the gospel texts through proclamation and through study, in part from the cultural bias toward Christianity that has itself been an outgrowth of Christianity, and in part from the sustenance of meaning and direction provided to us as we live in and from this knowledge. The God we see in Jesus Christ continues to act incarnationally for us and with us. And if the revelatory incarnation in Christ is symbolized through the lowly ambivalence of a manger, should it seem so strange that the continuing actions of God for us should be through such lowly and ambivalent incarnational means as texts, cultures, and personal histories?

The very ambivalence that mediates faith to us is an invitation to an active rather than passive appropriation of faith. If faith were mediated through absolutes of unquestioned clarity, then we might be believers, stamped by rote with correct belief, but we would hardly be faith-full. To be faith-full is to accept the challenge of ambivalence and ambiguity by coming to judgments and decisions. Incarnational Christianity calls us to participate in the forging of faith as well as the living of faith. For example, the very culture that makes it far more likely that we will be Christians rather than participants in an eastern faith such as Hinduism mediates unfaith as well as faith, and provides us with gross examples of structural injustice. The culture that is capable of being a mediator of faith must come under the judgment of faith, toward the end of its own transformation. This happens not through belief as a passive response to things received, but through the activity of faith taking the ambivalence even of the mediations of faith seriously. To trust a God whom we believe acts in and through our histories is not to rubber stamp our histories, but to sift them for their fullness, balancing them against texts and experience, discerning the incarnational activity of God.

Faith does not have to live from pretensions of universal truth, as if it were a God's-eye perspective; it is enough that we live from the more humbly-hewn faith of our own perspective. We presuppose the reality of God, and the presupposition is reinforced through our interpreted experience of this God who meets us in the midst of things.

So, then, our supposition is that it is indeed God that we know, and that the God that we know, knows us as well. But if we posit a provisional and partial nature to our own knowledge, we need not posit the same limitations to God. Rather, I suggest that were it not for the fullness of God's knowledge of the world, then the incarnational and providential work of God in the world would not be possible. And it is precisely the fullness of God's knowledge of the world that is the basis of maintaining that violation of the world is a violation of God as well. But this statement must be explicated further through the relational frame of reference that guides this entire investigation of sin.

The argument that existence is creation stems from a relational theology, rooted in a place within the Christian tradition deeply attuned to the relational heart of existence. I speak of flux and continuities, and dare to say that to be human is precisely to participate with some awareness in both the flux and continuity of ourselves, our construed worlds, and the environing earth. But the particular perspective from which I describe this flux and continuity comes from the relational philosophy of Alfred North Whitehead.

In this relational understanding, existence *is* creation in a threefold sense. Existence is continuously other-created, self-created, and God-created, without contradiction. It is other-created, in that the very process of existence requires a creative response to the vast multiplicity of influences bearing upon the becoming entity. Every element of existence is dynamic, having an effect, and that effect is in fact its influence on others. It is as if each existent thing were a unique center of energy, transmitting its energy to the wider universe. But there are many centers, and therefore many converging fields of energy. With each convergence there is the becoming of a new center, entering the process and adding its own unique energy to the many becoming fields. New events of becoming are as multiple as the universe itself—and, in fact, these becoming energies *are* the universe itself in its continuous process of reconstruing itself. Every existent thing emerges out of the dynamic force of converging energies.

Self-creation joins with other-creation. In the process of emerging, the new reality selectively unifies all the energies it has received into the peculiar configuration that is itself. This unification is the element of freedom within the entity—a conditioned freedom, to be sure, but freedom nonetheless, and the ground of saying that existence comes into being through the continuous process of creating itself.

Each reality emerges into being as a creative response to its particular past. It is shaped by that past, but transcends that past since it is a reconfiguration of the past in terms of the particular standpoint provided by the present. Every reality can be described in terms of 1) a receptive phase, wherein the convergent realities of its past evoke the selective process, 2) an integrative phase, wherein the past is creatively unified by the emerging subject, and 3) a projective phase, wherein the completed reality participates with the rest of the universe in calling new realities into being.

This description of reality is temporal, and can be correlated with the description of transcendence given in the previous chapter. The receptive phase relates to the past, and is the basis of memory. The projective phase relates to a future, and is the basis of imagination. The present is the interweaving of past and future into the uniqueness of present experience. It is the creative ground of empathy, since the otherness of the past is felt here, as present. The fullness of the present is at once an interpretation of the past, an experience of "withness," and a shaping influence upon a future yet to be. Thus all existence is inescapably relational, perspectival, and influential, and therefore all existence contains within itself the seeds of its own transcendence.

The present is the presence of the entity in its own creative integration of its past and its future. It integrates its past, insofar as the entity must selectively value the great multiplicity of influences it

receives, and hence assume responsibility for precisely how it becomes itself. The entity integrates its future insofar as its feelings
for what it might presently become guide its integration of the past.
Also, where consciousness is present, the event can include not only
the sense of its own becoming, but some sense of its future effects
upon others. These anticipations are woven into the present, and
can strongly influence how one responds to the past. But whether
we speak of the becoming of conscious or nonconscious creatures,
this whole process is an intense instance of creativity, so that creation
is creation partly through its own self-creativity. Creation is a process
that involves enormous creativity within that process. That which
we normally call "nature" is not inert, but incredibly active. Thus
whether one wishes to have reference to God or not, one legitimately calls nature creation.

But the third aspect whereby one legitimately names nature as
creation reflects a somewhat more traditional theological theme.
God's creativity interacts with the world's creativity. The world is a
welter of interrelating particles, with each emerging actuality responsible for unifying the multitudinous energies from its past.
Apart from some limiting factor, the magnitude of the past would
simply overwhelm creativity, producing but a sheer randomness of
energy. But a principle of limitation necessarily must relate to all
energies, and not just to some. A principle of limitation can only
operate effectively from its own comprehension of the entire complexity, and from some capacity for envisagement of what such energies, in various combinations, *can* become. This principle is God.
Insofar as God is a providential energy affecting every emerging
actuality as it copes with the problem of selectively integrating its
past, God is creator. This mode of creation, however, cannot be
wholly determinative, since it is a creative impulse or influence that
requires the becoming entity's response for actualization. Thus in
this relational ontology, God's creation of the world is a creation
with the world, rather than a simple creation *of* the world. And God's
mode of creation is through influence.

The sense in which existence is creation, then, is threefold, corres-
ponding in a sense with temporality. Since the creative energy of
God is a source of guidance, God's mode of creativity is through the
future. Since the becoming occasion emerges through the energies
emitted from the past, the other-creativity is through the past. Its
own self-creativity is the unification of past and future, and hence is

creativity in and through creation of itself as present. In the process, the world is constituted again and again and again as creation.

Clearly, there are enormous qualifications and implications hidden within these few paragraphs, but my purpose is not to give a full explication of what has been known as process philosophy, but to move more fully to an understanding of sin, its preconditions, and its effects. Insofar as intents or actions violate the well-being of creation, they are sins against creation, or a rebellion against creation's good. The sense in which the violation of creation is also a violation of God has to do with the relational sense of God's involvement in creation.

The traditional Whiteheadian way of saying that God influences each becoming entity of existence is to say that God provides an initial aim to every entity. Each entity emerges through its adaptation of this aim as the guiding force by which it integrates all of the influences that have called it into being. The becoming entity turns God's initial aim into its own subjective aim, and in the process, becomes itself.

Within process-relational thought, it is common to identify sin as deviation from God's initial aim. This relates closely to the traditional concept of sin as defying the limits that God has set for human existence. But this can be no more sufficient in a process-relational view than it is in a traditional view, given the complexity and even ambiguity of God's aims in a relational world. It is too simple to say that the adaptation of the initial aim is sin because 1) the intent of the aim must be influential rather than determinative; 2) the aim is already contextualized, so that it relates to the actual conditions in the world and not an idealized condition unrelated to that world; 3) the aim is not for a single good, but actually is more complex than that, and can imply multiple goods, each of which can yield different judgments in terms of what might be called "best"; 4) not all deviation from initial aims can be counted as sin. Therefore, another factor must be involved that marks some deviations as sinful, and I am arguing that this factor is unnecessary violence. When this is taken into view, the interpretation of sin as being against God becomes less what one has done with the aim of God, and more what one has done *to* God as God receives the effects of one's deeds into God's own experience. Sin is the unnecessary violation of well-being, and its occurrence in creation has an effect upon God. Because of this, sin against creation is also against God.

The influential nature of God's aim is due to the joint creativity between God and the world. The integrity of the world's self-creativity in response to the creativity of God is the real freedom, to whatever degree, of how it responds to all the forces, including God, that impinge upon it. In many cases, this freedom of response is the mere indeterminism that attends much phenomena. This indeterminism, in a relational world, is not simply due to the insufficiency of our measuring devices, but due to the responsive nature of that which we try to measure. Since all things have a dynamism within them, they respond to our measuring activity: we "know" them in their present responsiveness to this particular set of events, not in terms of what their responsiveness would have been to another series of events. This element of responsiveness is an element of variability, and hence is a form of indeterminism, however minute. The more complex an entity is, particularly as it participates in the complexity of life, the greater will be the degree of indeterminism. The maximum degree of indeterminism, known through our own experience, is freedom. But this continuum of bare indeterminism to freedom constitutes the real responsiveness of all events, and is why determinism, even from God, can never be absolute. Thus God's creative acts in the world are influential rather than deterministic, and one can presume that influential acts are not intended to be deterministic. Hence one concludes that God builds no essential requirement for absolute conformity into influential aims. Thus deviation from the initial aim alone cannot constitute sin.

The contextual nature of the aim gives further complexity to the situation. Whitehead noted that at times even the best of aims must be bad. There are situations where one must choose between evils, so that there is no purity, even to God's aims. A classic illustration is provided through the novel and later the film, *Sophie's Choice*.[2] One particular scene shows Sophie arriving at a concentration camp during World War II, leaving the freight car along with all the others, holding her small daughter, and clutching her son close to her side. The officer in charge of disposing of the prisoners, consigning some to death and others to work crews, confronts Sophie. After some conversation, he tells her that one of her children will be sent to death in the gas ovens immediately, and the other will be sent to a camp, and she, Sophie, must make the choice as to which child shall die, and which live. He tells her that if she does not choose, both children will be sent to immediate death. And then,

---

[2] William Styron, *Sophie's Choice* (New York: Random House, 1979).

with a smile, he asks her to choose. What kind of an "aim" could God provide Sophie at such a point, and how would one judge a "sinful" response? Does Sophie sin if she chooses her daughter instead of her son, or her son instead of her daughter? What could sin as "deviation from the aim of God" possibly mean for Sophie in such a moment of horror?

One could imagine all sorts of alternative situations, such as an officer who took pity on the woman and her children, and responded positively to God's presumed aim that he have mercy; one could imagine a world during 1943 that was not torn by war; one could imagine a world without camps designed for the ruthless extermination of peoples. But such imaginary alternatives are simply that. There were real "Sophies" during that period, albeit the Sophie of our illustration is fictional. The sin in the illustration is in the officer's direct violation of Sophie and her children, according to the criterion of well-being to be developed in our next chapter. If God is faitl ?ul, God must be with Sophie, offering her whatever best response is possible in her situation. But in no way can God's aim be "good," or its deviation, "sin." The context renders it a tragic aim, responsive to the tragedy of sin and evil in the world through which that aim must come.[3] The aims of God are contextual, mediated through God's feelings of the world, and thus there is no necessity that either clarity or purity be mediated through God's creative influence upon the world. In some cases even conformity to the aim of God embroils one in evil. How, then, can simple deviation from God's aim constitute sin?

Finally, the aim from God can relate to multiple goods, so that a choice for one rather than another opens up a whole new avenue of possibilities, and it is not always clear which avenue is best. For we not only live in a world where sometimes our context places us in the situation of choosing between multiple evils; we also can choose between multiple goods. To choose one over another is not sin. For example, a woman has chosen a career in law, and taken a position with a firm where she has the opportunity to contribute creatively to the firm's practice, and to develop her own skills as well. The firm is engaged in issues of environmental impact, and so she feels herself to be contributing to the good of society. Her

---

[3] Whitehead speaks of the initial aim as the "remorseless working of things" when "the best be bad" on page 244 of *Process and Reality* (New York: The Free Press, 1978; corrected edition edited by David Ray Griffin and Donald W. Sherburne).

reputation brings her to the attention of another firm that is also committed to ecological issues, and she receives an invitation to join that firm. How does she determine her best response? There will certainly be varying opinions as to which alternative will be "best" for her. How can she know God's best with regard to the alternative futures confronting her? Would she "sin against God" if she chose the "wrong" one? Perhaps it is more the case that she cannot make a wrong decision.

God will indeed offer guidance, but the guidance will not be in the form of a clear voice in the night, but in the form of options to weigh, factors to consider, friends to consult. She will have to make her own decision, cultivated with as much openness as possible to the variables of the situation. And whichever decision she makes, God will work with that choice, turning it into a "best" for her. God's guidance is not over and above the situation, but in and through the situation. Thus the limitations that God gives are constructive and flexible limitations rather than restrictive limitations; they are limitations that are contextualized in and through our world. The adaptation rather than adoption of God's aim is not necessarily a clear option, so that adaptation as opposed to adoption cannot automatically be construed as sin.

Thus the world is creation in and through its responses to the many influences evoking it into being—including the influence of God. We presume that the influence of God is toward interrelated communities of well-being. Violations of well-being most certainly occur, and these violations constitute a rebellion against the well-being of the world. In order to consider how these violations also are sins against God, we must go beyond looking at sin in relation to the initial aim of God, and consider sin in relation to its effects upon God. In violating the well-being of creation, sin also violates the well-being of God.

I have posited a relational world, composed of minute entities and aggregates of entities. The minute entities are the building blocks of dynamic responsive activity. They feel that which is other to themselves, integrate these influences into their own becoming, complete this integrative process, and so become influences on the future. These particles of energy form aggregates that become the basis of the organic and inorganic world we experience, including ourselves, and we fancy that human existence is that form of experience whereby the dynamic of all existence can be lifted first to consciousness, and then to self-consciousness. We live through the dim or sharp awareness that we are essentially and integrally related to all else on this earth, even though but a portion of those relationships enters into the daily variables through which we live, act, and constitute our being.

The role of God in this construal of a relational reality is integral, not fortuitous. God is posited as that "principle of limitation" that guides the responsiveness of entities within their contexts. In such a role, we can posit that God is indirectly responsible for human existence, for the conglomerate of chemicals that constituted our primeval earth millions of years ago presumably contained no inner need to move toward the development of homo sapiens. And in fact the earth appears to have done quite well for the vast majority of its existence without any such beings as ourselves. Dinosaurs seemed to satisfy the earth's creative urge toward complexity for a period of time far more vast than the epoch we humans have thus far achieved. But if God exercises a creative influence on the earth's own creative responses to existence, then we must posit that God did indeed lure the earth toward the emergence of our own species. Thus not only in the small sense of "initial aims" is God creator, but also in the larger sense of the evolution of the cosmos. Always, however, this needs to be interpreted not only in terms of God's influence, but also in terms of the earth's response.

The presupposition of God's creative influence is the fullness with which God knows the context from which the becoming entity emerges. But God can only know that context if in fact God relates to that context. And in a contextual universe, knowledge is an event wherein that which is known is connected to that which knows. A Whiteheadian way of putting it would be to say that knowledge is based on a transmission of feeling from one entity to another. This transmission of feeling is the way one entity feels another. Thus God not only has an influence upon the world, but this influence stems from the prior way in which the world has influenced God. God, like every other entity, feels the world; God's knowledge, like that of every other entity, is based upon the fullness of God's feelings. And this is the basis of saying that rebellion against the well-being of the world is always also a violation of God, who feels the world.

The role of God as creator requires God to feel the world. If God gives contextual guidance to the world, thus influencing the world's creativity, then God must know the context. God's knowledge of the context has proceeded through the world's return effect upon God.

To be, even for God, is to respond to all others and to have an effect upon all others. Thus God experiences the world's effect. Granted, to say this is to take the relational understanding of the world and to push it to its implications for the way God relates to the world, and as such, these statements are necessarily provisional, like all generalizations. Yet what they indicate is consistent with a relational world, and therefore can be taken as legitimate speculative implications for our understanding of God.

God not only affects the world, but is affected by the world. It is precisely because God is affected by the world that God can fashion guidance for the world. In a fully developed relational understanding, God is a singular reality presupposed by the very existence of the world, primordially existent. For metaphysical reasons made plain in Whitehead's works and its many expositions, the dynamics posited of God are the reverse of those evident in the world. The world proceeds from feelings of the past into integration of that past, and then into an influence upon the future. Thus the world, in all its constituent becoming parts, is essentially temporal. God "begins" primordially and therefore eternally in a decisive determination of the divine character through the ordered envisagement of all possibilities. From this determinate selfhood, God feels the world as it is, integrating these feelings judgmentally into the primordial divine character. From this integration, wherein God knows the world both as it is and as it can be, God feels possibilities for the ever-new becoming of the world in all of its various standpoints, in ways appropriate to those standpoints. The feelings for what the world can become grow 1) from the fullness of God's knowledge of the world's past, in all of its standpoints, which is the infinitely multiple contexts within the world, and 2) from the richness of possibilities in God's own envisagement of all possibilities within the divine nature. Thus the world moves from reception of influences to its own self-definition, whereas God moves from self-definition to reception of influences, or God's feelings of the world.

But if God feels the world, then God feels the world the way it is. When in fact the well-being of the world is violated, in any standpoint, God necessarily feels that violation. In the instances illustrated by the story of Sophie, God feels Sophie's agony with her, and on the basis of that co-feeling, feels what forms of transformation are yet possible for her *in these circumstances*. These forms of transformation include a transcendent integration of God's feelings of Sophie within the divine nature, as well as the historical possibilities, however tragic they must be. God's co-feeling with Sophie means that in violating Sophie, the officer has violated God as well. Because God feels the world, and the world as it is has an effect upon God, rebellion against creation entails sin against God. But it is sin against God *because* it is a rebellion against creation.

One necessarily also posits that God feels the officer, including whatever sadistic satisfaction the officer feels through his torment of Sophie. But since God, in this projection, feels the world in relation to its wider context (e.g., Sophie's suffering and the children's terror), the feeling of the officer's satisfaction is contextualized by pain, and thus is received as judgment. Furthermore, God feels each instance of the world not only in relation to its context, but in relation to the divine character, in which case God feels the officer judgmentally in terms of the officer's violation of God's own nature. But just as Sophie is felt toward the end of transformation, even so the officer would be felt toward the end of transformation. The officer, too, has a trajectory that creates itself in response to the aims of God. But his deviation from the aim of God is not the fundamental problem of sin. Rather, only when that deviation itself aims at the unnecessary violation of well-being is there sin. The chosen trajectory toward violence takes precedence over well-being, overriding or muting the transformative aim of God. Thus the nature of the sin is primarily defined in relation to the well-being of creation, and not simply on the basis of an authoritarian command of God. Sin is rebellion against creation, violating the world's well-being. In so doing, it also necessarily violates God's well-being. The suffering of the world entails the suffering of God.

These comments have taken a fictionalized account of sin as an example, but the news report leading this chapter gives a factual account of racism, political murder and the attendant suffering within all segments of South African society. These sins are focused in South Africa, but cannot be confined to that locale. They not only affect the whole world; they also affect God, since God feels the experiences of all within the society, internalized within a divine compassion that is not simply intellectual, but is instead the depths of a feeling-with.

Earlier I cited violations in another community. That news account spoke of a veterinarian murdered before his wife and daughter, of a host of Muslims slain, and of the death of a seventeen-year-old Serbian girl. The murderers sinned against those they killed, the townspeople, the religious communities involved, and themselves. Their acts were direct rebellions against the well-being of creation. In the light of the concept of God developed in this chapter, I can also say that these rebellions against creation were also sins against God. God, too, experienced the bullets, the knife; God, too, experienced the helplessness in the witnesses; God, too, experienced the brutalized humanity of the aggressors. God, too, was violated.

Central in Christian symbolism is a cross, where the one called the incarnation of God suffered and died through human violence. If God co-experiences the experiences of the world, then our identification of God with Christ on the cross suggests that every sin is a sin not only against creation, but also against God. The sin is not a primal violation of a command, but a primal violation of well-being. Given this, one muses about cautioning Christians against making the political torture on a cross more central than the Easter theme of resurrection, for the torture bespeaks the violence of human viciousness, while the resurrection bespeaks the transforming power of God.

Before examining the origins and transmission of sin as a violation of well-being, it is essential to address the criterion of well-being itself. In a world where sin is defined as rebellion against God, the criterion of sin is that which goes against God's will. In a world where sin is defined as the violation of well-being, then the criterion against which sin is measured is well-being. In this case, violation of a command is judged as sinful not because the command has been violated, but because the well-being encoded within the command has been violated. But what is that well-being, and how is it determined? We turn now to this issue.

SIN

A 53-year-old Santa Monica grocer was shot and killed Tuesday night when he resisted a gunman's attempt to rob him on a street that police say used to be one of Encino's safest.

Police said the victim . . . was parked in his Honda Civic just before midnight Tuesday when a stranger used a pistol to smash the passenger window. The gunman shot [the victim] once in the head . . . [He] died at the scene, which is in front of his apartment building.

Violent crime once was unheard-of in the neighborhood, "but in the last year or two, we've had three [robbery-related] murders in that four-block area."

—*Los Angeles Times*
Thursday, September 2, 1993

4

THE CRITERION
OF WELL-BEING

S in is a rebellion against creation in the unnecessary violation of the well-being of any aspect of existence. Because it is a violation of creation, it is also sin against God.

But what is the criterion that establishes "violation"? If sin works "ill-being," then clearly some concept of "well-being" is required, but what constitutes well-being? Furthermore, if sin is to be defined primarily as rebellion against the well-being of any aspect of existence, then the criterion needs to be located within the whole of existence. Part of the difficulty with the notion of sin as rebellion against God is that sin then becomes that which goes against the will of God, so that the criterion of sin is not within creation, but within God. Hence any violation of this criterion is immediately a rebellion against God. To change the definition of sin requires a change in the criterion that measures sin. The work of this chapter will be to demonstrate that the well-being of the world and of God and the world together is established through interdependence, and that ultimately interdependence requires an inclusiveness of well-being. Inclusive well-being is therefore the norm against which sin is measured.

My method for establishing this criterion has recourse to the need that it be rooted within the whole of existence. The development of the last two chapters defines that whole not as the world alone, nor as God alone, but as God and the world together in an interrelated, interdependent whole. Consequently, I will explore a criterion of well-being based first on the interdependence within the world, second on the notion of a relational God, and third on the togetherness of God and the world. This will be in keeping with the thesis that sin is a rebellion against creation that also violates God.

If the well-being of creation constitutes the norm against which one measures sin, then we are thrown into an area with both problems and possibilities. The problems are: 1) Life is robbery, as Whitehead noted.[1] All life, and not just human life, lives through the destruction of other life, whether that other be animal or vegetable. How can "well-being" serve as a concept for measuring sin, if in fact our very existence depends upon the destruction, and therefore the ill-being, of other life? 2) "Well-being" is a culturally dependent concept; how is it to serve the purpose of being a criterion? Or is sin in fact a culturally limited concept, with no application between cultures?

But the possibility of a criterion of well-being is the visionary dream expressed in the remarkable phrase of Julian of Norwich: "That all shall be well, and all shall be well, and all manner of things shall be well." The dream and the issues named above are in tension, but the tension itself is essential for understanding well-being and therefore sin in a relational, interdependent world.

The vision of well-being speaks minimally of a human world where the basic essentials for existence such as nourishment and shelter are available, and are also supplemented by the opportunity for labor, meaning, and emotional nourishment. While such a description of well-being most clearly has reference to the human community, the "all" of the "shall be well" goes beyond the human sphere to the whole range of interdependent existence, both organic and inorganic. The "all" is comprehensive. But the "all" is given from a certain perspective. To see a vision of well-being is to see from a certain standpoint and particularity. We are each one of us centers of an existence that is many-centered.

Nor can we presume that human centering and human perspective exhaust the centered perspectives of the world we construe and know. Relationships with animals teach us of centering and perspective within other forms of being, and this knowledge extends to include the creatures of the sea. Relationships with plants and trees extend the realm of centering to include these forms of life as well, although we do not presume their consciousness. But they

---

[1] A.N. Whitehead, *Process and Reality*, p. 105.

live, and respond, and thrive or decline not simply in terms of a given life span, but also in terms of factors in their environments that make for their well or their ill-being. Beyond these is the realm of insect life, sometimes our bane, sometimes our blessing, and sometimes simply our co-existents on this earth, but contributing and responding in their various ways to the wholeness of life. Beyond our ordinary visual or audial perceptive abilities is yet the micro world of bacteria and viruses, and creatures one hardly knows how to classify as life or nonlife. Sustaining us all is the environing earth, air, fire, and water. Every perspective is a true perspective, "true north" in a teeming world of centerless centering. We see perspectivally, in spiraling circles ever extending beyond our own center, circles that exist through their myriad modes of centering. And the impossible yearning is that through all the spiraling centers of existence, all shall be well, and all shall be well, and all manner of things shall be well.

The many centers are not strangers to one another, but exist in patterns and structures that are both like and unlike. Lewis Thomas, in his delightful classic, *Lives of a Cell*,[2] humorously describes the fascination of New Yorkers as they flock to see the amazing spectacle of a termite colony, lifted intact from the Amazon and brought to Manhattan for the edification of museum goers. As the bemused observers marvel at the routinized order of the colony, Thomas moves the camera of his description further and further away, so that we see first the museum as a whole, then that portion of the city that holds the museum, and finally a view of the whole termite-like colony that is New York. Our interdependence is our mirroring of one another, our similarities of sharing in structures that organize our spaces and times. We are like, even while we are unlike.

Our interdependence is our mutual reliance upon one another. Again from Lewis Thomas comes a graphic description of the peculiarity of the human organism, which is not one body, but many. The health of the body depends upon the work of the colonies of bacteria living within us, so that from our perspective the bacteria exist within us for the sake of our well-being, but of course, one could also say that we exist as "world" for such bacteria, and we are therefore necessary for their well-being. Who exists for whom? And our own embodiment is but one more illustration from many within

2 Lewis Thomas, *Lives of a Cell: A Biologist Looks at Life* (New York: Bantam Press, 1974).

our interdependent world, where each is a relative center, and none is an absolute center. We exist in a universe of centerless centering, and in such a universe we are not fortuitously interdependent, but necessarily so.

An "El Niño" phenomenon warms the surface waters of the Pacific Ocean, interfering with the production of the plankton that supports the krell that support the whales, as well as a myriad chain of other creatures that ultimately depend upon the favorable production of plankton. On land, a drought affects the water table that supports the vegetation that supports the life of vast acres of land. Interdependence is the very stuff of life.

Interdependence is the basis not simply of physical life, but of emotional life as well. Infants and children are nourished not only by food, but also by caring attention, by arms that hold, voices that sing, and faces that smile. Through such nourishment, the spirit grows as the infant returns the smile, reaching out to touch and to hold in return. Hospitals have long since learned that premature infants who are held and given positive emotional care grow faster and have fewer physical problems than the same kinds of infants who are left in machines that effectively tend to their physical needs, but leave unaddressed the emotions. Our spirits grow through the entwining affection we receive and give. Loving emotional interdependence is the stuff that makes for spirit; its lack is the stunting or perversion of spirit.

To view the fullness of interdependent existence perspectivally inevitably creates gradations of valuing this interdependence. We tend to value most those upon whom we depend the most, whether for our spiritual or physical well-being. One cares about the plight of starving children in distant lands, but one is more often galvanized to immediate action by the hunger of one's own child. We care about the ability to find cures for dreadful diseases in general, but when one in our own family is stricken, our general care takes on poignant urgency. Our emotions leave no doubt that we value the continued health of our loved one over the "health" of whatever bacterial or viral or cancerous life form is endangering the life we love. This familial love is easily extended when the scientific issue is raised as to whether the last live sample of smallpox virus should be saved. We would rather see it destroyed than risk its continued power to destroy again the life of any human being, whether friend or stranger. To be centered, then, means that we inevitably see and value things from the perspective of our center in relation to the continued well-being of ourselves and those within the spiraling circles of interdependence closest to us.

Yet the facticity of our interdependence is that it is not possible to draw the spiral of our own interdependence to a close short of including the whole universe. We experience gradations of value depending upon whether something is necessarily food for us, so that we cut down the plant, or kill the animal—or, as in the case of the virus, we are necessarily food for something else, in which case we do our best to cut down that something else. It is not possible to value things equally in an interdependent world, where we exist in and through one another and in and through an environment; we value from our perspective. But given the scope of our interdependence, our perspective has fuzzy edges, and boundaries that in fact are ever receding.

The argument that interdependence entails mutual responsibility is based upon the assumption that well-being is a value for every centered existent. As persons, said Whitehead, we desire to live, to live well, and to live better. Pathologies sometimes interfere with this desire, as in the case of those who, never having received love, do not know how to love themselves and therefore do not desire to live. But the norm by far is that each does desire his or her own well-being. One's well-being, however, depends upon the well-being of others, whether that otherness relates to the physical, animal, or human world.

Interdependence implies reciprocal relations of well-being. The situation is negatively illustrated through the news account concerning a man murdered in front of his home. Well-being depends upon one's sense of safety, which in turn depends upon a reasonable trust in others. The murderers of the grocer and the earlier victims not only destroyed life; they also destroyed the reasonable trust in the good will of others that creates neighborhood. Neighborhoods are built not only on mutual regard among residents, but also on the assumption that one's own neighborhood is but one of many like-minded communities. The break-down of this trust is the violation of well-being in many forms. And the violation of well-being is sin.

An interdependent world is a world beyond egoism or altruism, since every centered self exists in and through relations to other centered selves. Simply put, we do not stop with our skin; we involve a network of relations spiraling out beyond ourselves. Thus the responsibility to self and others is not exactly "enlightened self-interest," since it could just as easily be called "enlightened other-interest." We are interwoven. In this interwovenness, interdependence combined with the urge toward well-being equals responsibility for the well-being of self and others. This responsibility is as extensive as relationships. But while immediate relationships are obvious, they are by no means exhaustive—our relationality finally draws us into connection with the entire universe.

Thus far, I have spoken of interdependence and reciprocal responsibility primarily from the perspective of personal existence. But given the complexity and extensiveness of interdependence, it is not possible to respond to all relationships on a personal level. In an ideal interdependent world one would hope that every centered form of existence would experience its own circles of caring. Yet whether through the violence of sin or through the fortunes of nature, it is manifestly not the case that every center of existence receives and gives that which is required for well-being from those relations nearest to it. Therefore, we depend upon our social structures and societies to mediate care to those beyond the scope of personal relation. In the Hebrew scriptures, the needy are symbolized through the widow, the orphan, and the stranger, and laws were formulated to create the social structures that could mediate care to them.

Yet even in the best of worlds, where such structures are capable of mediating physical needs, the emotional needs of persons cannot be met by impersonal structures. Thus neither personal caring nor institutional caring is sufficient to address fully the interdependent needs of all persons. Furthermore, since the capacities of personal caring are not broad enough even to extend to mutual care toward all persons, then clearly the capacity to care equally for all living things, let alone all things whatsoever, is likewise restricted. The paradox obtains, then, that while the actuality of interdependence is as wide as the universe, and therefore responsibility for well-being is likewise extensive, the competitive needs for life, the selective function of consciousness, and the impersonal nature of social structures make tenuous any insurance of universal well-being. We are left with small circles of personal caring, which is both a giving and a receiving in gradations of intensity, and with structures that may include within their purpose the wider caring for society, persons, and nature, again with varying degrees of intentionality and intensity. Whether personal or socially structured, this relational care is perspectival, with a consequent hierarchy of values that rates the human above other forms of existence. Thus the ideal of universal well-being and the responsibility for such well-being, while rooted in the universality of relations, is one that is incapable of full realization either personally or structurally, due to limitations of finitude and of perspective.

And yet at the root of being is the raw fact that in an interdependent world, the well-being of one depends in some sense on the well-being of all. The previous familial illustration can be supplemented with an example from the environment, such as in the case of a river that provides drinking water for a people. If the water is polluted, then it becomes infested with bacteria that are dangerous for many forms of life, including human life. The well-being of the people, then, requires the well-being of the river. And the clear flow of the river depends upon the forestation along its banks, and the fish within its waters. Whether it be a totally human judgment or no to say that the river is "well" when its waters flow purely and freely, and that the river is "ill" when its waters no longer support many forms of life, the facticity of the situation is that the chain of well-being based on the purity of the waters includes life forms other than human, so that well-being is a mutual concept, and not a restrictive concept. Because of interdependence, the actual dependence upon others' well-being is far greater than that which we are capable of embracing within our consciousness. Interdependence is universal; the requirements for well-being are likewise universal.

One might argue that, from the perspective of the bacteria that thrive in the polluted waters, a whole different chain of well-being emerges that is in competition with that chain which supports more complex forms of life. The response from the perspective of human life is that where and when possible, all forms of life should thrive, but the reality of the human center creates for us a priority for the well-being of complex life forms over those which seem to us to be incapable of supporting consciousness. To acknowledge one's own perspective is to recognize the gradations of value that belong to that perspective. The tension, however, is that competing value systems and life forms always raise the question to one's perspective, asking to what extent one's grades of value are too small, to what extent they might be enlarged. If in fact interdependence is as wide as the universe, the questions raised to our particular limitations are potentially also as wide as the universe.

Thus we hold to a criterion of well-being—that *all* shall be well—even while recognizing that but a small proportion of that "all" enters into our active care and concern, and that some of that "all" even poses a threat to our own well-being. Should we not give up the very notion of universal well-being, then, in admitted favor of the particular well-being that pertains to our own perspective? Despite the impossibility attached to the ideal, there is yet a pragmatic function to the ideal. Since we are limited in our caring capacities, and since our institutions are in some ways more limited (and in other ways more effective), we are always in danger of drawing our line of caring more narrowly than necessary, and more solidly than the spiraling circle of actual interdependence supports. To hold to a criterion of universal well-being, despite its problems, is always to hold before us a question concerning the limits that we otherwise so comfortably draw. History and our own lives well show us how easily we draw the line of well-being around those closest to us— all the while, since we receive from all else and affect all else, actually contributing to the ill-being of those beyond our closed borders. To hold to a criterion of *universal* well-being challenges every border we close, and ever raises before us the reality that in fact our interdependence is far wider than we can consciously know. Therefore, in spite of all the qualifications and difficulties, the impossible ideal of universal well-being is the most effective. It provides an ideal that calls our more limited ideals ever into question, and in the process holds the possibility of bringing our intentions and our caring into greater conformity with the interdependence through which we find our being.

If we stop with a criterion of universal well-being based on the interdependence of existence, we have not yet dealt with *all* of existence, given the supposition essential to this inquiry that God exists. The relational notion of God presented in the previous chapter posits a God intimately related to the world, so that a concept of universal well-being must also include the well-being of God. When a relational understanding of God is included in the criterion of universal well-being, then the interdependence that makes for well-being is supplemented with qualities of truth, love, and beauty. For these qualities are essential to the well-being of God.

"That all shall be well, and all shall be well, and all manner of things shall be well." Dame Julian's provocative statement stemmed from her own mystical sense of the union of all things with God. A relational view also posits a dynamic union of all things with God in an interactive flow of time and everlastingness.

The relational understanding of God posits God as the one reality who relates to every creaturely existent whatsoever. While the crea-

ture does have an internal relation to every item in its entire universe, that universe does not include the entities of the future, nor
even the contemporaries of the entity. Every entity has an actual
universe that differs to a greater or lesser extent from every other
actual universe. Each bit of actuality emerges in a particular locus
that defines its universe from an unrepeatable perspective. And if
each emerges from a universe slightly different from all others to
begin with, the unique perspective of the entity further differentiates that universe in its own experience. Finally, the universe so
experienced is limited to the entities within the past—the present
entity will be included in its successor universes, but it cannot include that future within itself. In this sense, then, there is no "the
universe" save in abstraction, for that which we call "the universe"
is different from every standpoint and every perspective, and is
continually in the process of succeeding itself.

But the entity that is God spans all times, grounds all times, includes all times. God relates to every element in the universe, first
by influencing each element in its own becoming, and second by
feeling it upon its conclusion. God and only God is the one reality
that is capable of feeling the universe as it is, in each of its incredibly
multiple states.

Within this relational conceptuality, God internally feels the universe in all its multiplicity. God's feelings are not external affairs,
unrelated to the being of God. And in fact, if God feels the world,
and if the world is continuously adding new entities, then God's
feelings of the world are a continuous dynamism within God, consti-
tuting God as also in some sense becoming. For God to feel the
world is for God to recreate the world within the divine self, and
to integrate those feelings of the world into the divine character.

Such an integration would necessarily be judgmental and salvific.
Because the God who feels the multiplicity of the world is one, God
would feel each aspect of the world in relation to all other aspects.
Further, God would feel each aspect in relation to the initial influence God had offered that entity, feeling the difference between
what the entity could have been and what the entity became. Finally,
God would feel the entity relative to God's own character. Each of
these modes of feeling is at the same time a judgment upon the
felt entity, so that God's feelings of the world are not indiscriminate,
but discriminate, judgmental. The judgment, of course, is contextual, relational, and therefore it is a true judgment.

The salvific aspect of the judgment would be first of all its truth, second its love, and finally its beauty. In terms of truth as salvific, the distortions that mitigate against well-being would be impossible in God. In the haunting words of the apostle Paul, "Now we see through a glass, darkly; then we shall see face to face. Now we know in part, then shall we know even as also we have been known."

In terms of love, if love involves an ultimate acceptance of the other as the other really is, then God's love becomes a standard for all other forms of love, for God and only God has the ability to know the other as the other really is, and this knowledge is at the same time acceptance, even in judgment. God includes the otherness of the world within God's very being, even while accepting that otherness in the fullness of itself.

In terms of beauty, God's feeling of the world is not simply for the sake of feeling the world, nor even of judging the world, nor even of loving the world. But God's feeling, judgment, and love of the world are for the sake of integrating the world into God's own nature as the final adventure of things in a harmony that continuously surpasses itself, and this is beauty.

But of course truth, love, and beauty are finally all aspects of one another. God is not first truth, then love, and then beauty, but God is always truth, always love, and always beauty. On the one hand they would be continuous moments in the divine life, but on the other hand they would be always passing into each other in the divine life. On the one hand, it would be the reception of the world into God's being that constitutes God as truth, love, and beauty, but on the other hand it is God's self-determined character that constitutes such a reception of the world as truth, love, and beauty. Thus God's feeling of the world is the "material" through which God everlastingly becomes the divine self, and the divine self is ever given to the "material" that is the received world.

The vision of a relational God, then, is a vision of truth, love, and beauty, and it is these three that finally constitute the well-being of the world as well as God. The relational God, as was noted in the last chapter, is not simply a receiving God, but a giving God. God gives to every element of the world. Earlier I spoke of this giving as contextual, incarnational, so that God offers to every element in the world that which best meets its condition. This "best" is a combination of that which the actual world actually affords that standpoint, and whatever of the divine character that particular standpoint can bear.

If God relates to an entity within a molecule of dust, then the possibilities for that emerging entity are very much conditioned by whatever it is that makes for dust. The capacity of the emerging entity for transcendence is slight, which means that the imprint of the divine character on the mote of dust will likewise be minimal. If God relates to an entity emerging in the center of human personality, then that guiding relationship will be contextualized by the various gradations of the person's past. Human personality, stabilized by the environs of bodied existence, is open to greater novelty than is the entity within the molecule of dust, and hence human personality is more open to the effect of the character of God on one's context.

But what God is, is the transformation of the immediate past world within the depths of the divine truth, love, and beauty. In that case, what is done in heaven is of immediate concern on earth, for if God is received contextually, then the fullness of that context has to include what in fact has happened in God. Thus the transformation of the world in God is relevant for the possible transformation of the newly becoming world in history. If in God there is a reality where all is well, and all is well, and all manner of things are finally well, then there is made possible in every moment of human history an echoing way in which all may be well, and all may be well, and all manner of things may be well.

In considering the criterion of well-being relative to God, we are led to an understanding of an ultimate truth, love, and beauty pertaining to all things. In considering the criterion of well-being from the perspective of existence in the world, we are led to well-being as a necessary ideal, even while it is an ideal impossible of full instantiation from the point of view of a single person. It is a call to responsibility that nonetheless exceeds the practical ability of any one person, or any one human system. But before expanding this issue into a detailed consideration of what we might mean by original sin in an interdependent world, there is yet one more aspect of the criterion of well-being that must be examined, and that has to do with considering the two foci of God and the world together. How do the truth, love, and beauty that form a criterion for universal well-being in God combine with the universal responsibility for well-being that emerges simply from a consideration of interdependence? For the supposition is that the reality of things is not of a God and of a world in isolation, but of a God and a world that together add to each others' richness in an ultimate interdependence.

The operative understanding of the interdependence between God and the world is that God experiences the world in and through each entity that continuously makes up the world. But if God experiences *each* entity, and if each entity is affected by the many that have preceded it, then God and only God knows fully that with which each entity deals. For God has already experienced in their own times the many elements now affecting the becoming creature. Relative to persons, a person is not simply one entity, but a compound organism of many entities that supports one continuously self-succeeding center of consciousness. God not only experiences the past of a person, but God also experiences the full complexity of personhood. God experiences all of the entities making up that organism, and therefore also feels the person as a whole. This is particularly pertinent for God's feeling of the very centeredness of the person, which we might call the person's soul. Upon every moment of its moment-by-moment completion, God feels and therefore knows the self. But this divine experiential knowledge is not limited to persons; it extends to the fullness of every element of creation.

This experiential knowledge of the world issues into a responsiveness to the world. This responsiveness is conditioned by the world, by God's own nature of truth, love, and beauty, and by the possibilities for the future of the world from each finite perspective. This means, then, that insofar as the interdependent world reaches toward well-being, the form of this well-being will in fact be conditioned by the nature of God, whether dimly or brightly. Truth, love, and beauty will qualify the ideal of worldly well-being. Thus the criterion of well-being is not simply idiosyncratically defined, so that well-being in one corner of the universe has no integral relation to well-being in another corner of the universe. All elements in the universe experience the responsiveness of God, and this responsiveness echoes not only the contextuality of that portion of the universe, but also the contextuality of God. Therefore, God's truth, love, and beauty are adapted to the myriad circumstances of the universe. In this case, well-being anywhere will exhibit and contribute to truth, love, and beauty.

But what is truth, what is love, what is beauty? The enormous literature written in response to such a question is witness enough to the great diversity of ways in which these can be interpreted. In a relational world, where these qualities are infinitely adaptable to the infinite circumstances of the world, the relativity attending to these qualities is sufficient to support a literature even more vast than that already produced. But the fact that truth, love, and beauty can be manifested in an infinity of forms does not negate the singularity of their source in God, and therefore does not negate their value as a contextualized standard qualifying well-being.

Truth, in this context, is God's absolute knowledge of every entity in the fullness of what it has become. The application of this quality to human life means that despite the mystery of the self even to its own self, one is known. To be absolutely known is to be in absolute relation, even in a relative world. Love, in this context, is God's absolute acceptance of every entity in the fullness of what it can be, both within God's transforming action within the divine reality, and within the ongoing world. The application of this quality to human life means that the fullness with which one is known is in the mode of love, and that this love is therefore at the same time the demand for one's well-being. One is loved toward one's good, and toward one's relational good.

Beauty, in this context, is God's ability to integrate every entity not only with all others in a "reconciliation of all things" within God's own nature, but also with the infinite resources of the divine harmony. God, continuously experiencing the world from God's own perspective of truth and love, is an infinitely self-surpassing panorama of beauty constantly succeeding itself. The application of this quality to human life means that one's well-being has an essential openness to it whereby it can weave more and more forms of otherness into itself and to a degree into its self-awareness. One receives sight beyond the narrow form of familiar beauty, one can be broken open to beauties not hitherto known, to the infinite enrichment of the self and therefore of the self for others.

But if these are applications of the effect of God upon well-being in the world, note that these effects qualify well-being, but do not exhaust it. Truth, love, and beauty as expressed in one culture may seem quite strange to someone unfamiliar with that culture, whose sensitivities are molded by a different context. More drastically, that which is truth, love, and beauty in one culture may seem to contradict that which is known in another—and, in fact, may contradict it. An example would be a Christian and a Hindu understanding of well-being. To a Christian, well-being most certainly includes having one's basic physical needs met. But to a Hindu, whose religious perspective is oriented to a series of lifetimes rather than toward a single lifetime, a life of suffering may in fact represent a form of well-being. The violation of truth and love and beauty in one life may have incurred a debt of karma that could only be worked out in another life, so that the present life of suffering is in fact a cleansing of that old debt, making ready a further life in better circumstances. The Christian might demand that the suffering be alleviated. And the Hindu might respond that to do so would inculcate yet further bad karma, leading to even worse circumstances in the next life. The criterion of well-being through truth, love, and beauty requires that one work out the karma through suffering, not that one interrupt the karma with supposed but quite short-sighted contemporary "well-being." How is God's truth, love, and beauty equally represented in the Christian and the Hindu view?

There may be no resolution short of heated debate over the immediate issues. But it is quite plausible that in a world where finite existence in harsh circumstances does indeed create suffering, and where the relatively recent discoveries of medicine and sanitation were or are not readily available, that a helpful way to deal with that suffering is to give it a reason and a goal. Indeed, the reason can be perverted to justify suffering, even as in Christianity many a religious reason has been devised to justify suffering, such as with slavery or witch burning. But the argument over what constitutes well-being must be focused not on the reason given for the suffering, but on the ideal represented by the goal. If present suffering is for the sake of eventual well-being, what constitutes the fullness of that eventual well-being? That is, each religious system and/or cultural system tends toward endorsement of some idealized form of well-being, and it is in that teleological or eschatological formulation that the recognizable marks of truth, love, and beauty will be found.

The contextuality of the world means that truth, love, and beauty will be manifested in many varieties of well-being, and will even be used as a rationale for that which contradicts truth, love, and beauty. But the contextuality of a God who is truth, love, and beauty, and who relates to the world in every aspect of its existence, means that the divine truth, love, and beauty will have their traces throughout the universe.

The criterion itself calls for an openness to many forms. If truth, love, and beauty in God's own nature are such that they create a dynamic reality, always surpassing itself, then surely no finite mode of truth, love, and beauty can be final. Every form can be transcended, for every form is but one form in an infinite variety of forms.

Thus the criterion of well-being is not empty, nor is it so varied as to be necessarily unrecognizable. To the degree that well-being is violated, to the degree that human conduct negates the truth of the other's or one's own fullness, to the degree that human conduct has no love toward the other's or one's own good; to the degree that human conduct maintains a blindness to beauty in forms other than one's own, to that degree there is sin. Sin is the violation of the well-being of creation.

SIN

Children are routinely tortured and killed or arbitrarily detained by police in many countries around the world, Amnesty International said Wednesday. Its report, "Innocence Betrayed: Human Rights Violations Against Children and Young People," describes the slaying of street children in Brazil by vigilante squads and the brutal detention of youngsters in India. Other examples include a sixteen year old Kurdish girl who died in Turkish police custody, her body showing signs of extensive torture. A Mexican teenager is said to have been so savagely tortured that he hardly had the strength to react to his toenails being pulled out. Some children are deliberately targeted for human rights abuses because they are seen as social or political threats; others have been detained or tortured in order to force surrender or confession from their parents," the report said.

—*Los Angeles Times*
Monday, March 29, 1993

PART 2
THE STRUCTURE OF ORIGINAL SIN

CHAPTER

5

SIN THROUGH VIOLENCE

To restate the problem, original sin defined the human situation as one of universal implication in sin, apart from any conscious consent. Sins arise from the condition of sin. Whether classical theologians dealt with the nature of sin as pride, sloth, unbelief, disobedience, or any other variation, the exercise of all vices depended upon and arose from this original condition. The mechanism used to account for the universal nature of sin was the first humans' misdirected will in deviating from their given good. With this deviation, they corrupted the nature that was passed on to their progeny. Every generation consequently finds itself in the plight that it must deal with an internal inclination to participate in and therefore to perpetuate sin. Original sin begets sinners.

In our contemporary situation we experience an enormity to social and personal evils, but the notion of "original sin" that accounts for them theologically has been brought into question. Issues such as racism, sexism, classism, heterosexism, handicappism, anthropocentrism, anti-semitism, and whatever other "isms" we have devised toward the ill-being of peoples and nature, together with massive machines of organized killing called wars and ever more awesome capacities to destroy our environment, require more than an analysis of individual sin to account for the pervasiveness and depth of the problem. The doctrine of original sin must be reappropriated in such a way that it speaks to our condition, and allows us to name our condition.

As noted in the discussion of Reinhold Niebuhr, anxiety plays a major role in twentieth century discussions of original sin. In such thinking, all sin stems from the need to secure oneself from the anxieties of existence. Thus the fundamental reason why men rape women, or soldiers commit atrocities, or adults abuse children, is because such people are acting out of an anxiety triggered by their finitude and consequent insecurity.

Yet this seems to put too heavy a burden upon the human phenomenon of finitude, nor does it take into consideration the positive elements of anxiety. In many respects anxiety is an important if painful aspect of our humanity resulting from the vulnerability of relationships. To love a person who is in imminent danger of death, such as one with a terminal illness, is to be subjected to anxiety over the well-being of the loved one. The anxiety also contributes to one's anguish in such a situation, but would it be better to feel no anguish? Surely anguish over the pain of the other and over the impending loss are natural consequences of love. And far from becoming a direct path to sin, the anxiety that underlies this anguish often becomes the prompting power for acts of kindness and care. Likewise, persons facing their own imminent death often respond to the attendant anxiety not by increased sinning, but by increased albeit anguished value of the beauty of all the ordinarinesses of life, and by an overflow of love toward those they hold dear. Since Niebuhr and others consider the fragility of life to be the limiting factor causing anxiety, surely the condition of those most directly confronted with death should be illustrations of the power of anxiety as the presupposition of sin. But this is not the case.

As for anxiety over the lack of being a self, is it anxiety that produces the lack of being a self or the other way around? Feminists and minority scholars amply show that society pressures or forces selected groups into pre-established roles that have no necessary relation to the unique capabilities of the persons concerned. Under such conditions, it is eminently difficult to break out of these roles in order to discover and develop one's true bent, or, as feminists put it, "one's own voice." Is it not the case that the lack of a "self" imposed by such conditions is itself the cause of anxiety? Furthermore, far from anxiety then becoming a condition influencing one to sin, anxiety can become the catalyst that signals the wrongness of the stereotype into which one is forced. Anxiety can be a first step toward liberation.

It seems specious to argue that those who oppress children and young people, such as is recounted in the Amnesty International report at the beginning of this chapter, do so out of a fundamental anxiety occasioned by their mortality. Is all domination, greed, rapaciousness, and cruelty so reducible to the need to shore up the defenses against death? To the contrary, young persons often (though certainly not always) seem so unaware of their mortality as to be overly incautious, and even the phenomenon of teen-age suicide is tinged with the haunting tragedy that the victims do not really believe in death. Adults also can be marvelously impervious to mortality so long as they are healthy, and the shock of serious illness is often the surprised recognition that "even I am mortal." How, then, is anxiety over fear of death to account for the extent and enormity of sins of oppression?

To be sure, some theologians such as Paul Tillich dismiss anxieties over specific things, such as imminent death or the lack of oneself, as being but bare manifestations of a far deeper "existential anxiety" that in fact has no object. This type of anxiety emerges concomitantly with one's finitude, and is the natural response to finitude. But when one attempts to balance the enormity of sin with an anxiety engendered by finitude, then the scales crash down on the side of sin. Given the insufficiency of experienced anxiety relative to death to account particularly for sin, how can an underlying anxiety over finitude per se be the prompting cause of all human evil? One wonders if such existential anxiety is a phantom called up to save the notion of "rebellion against God" as the primal notion of sin. Anxiety over one's finitude, whether occasioned by nameable situations or by an unnameable existential precondition of human personality, seems a fragile beast to bear the burden of so enormous a problem as human violence.

Rather than looking to a finitude-engendered anxiety as the reason behind human ill-doing, why not look to a violence-engendered anxiety? It might well be that human personality contains a substructure of violent aggression related to survival, and that the effects of this substructure give rise to an anxiety such as Tillich named. Violence rather than finitude per se is the presenting cause of anxiety. This suggestion will be developed more fully in chapter six; for the present, we explore the issue of the human tendency toward violence as the condition of sin. My thesis is that original sin is created through a triadic structure constituted by a propensity toward violence, by an interrelational solidarity of the human species, and by social structures that shape the formation of consciousness and conscience.

With regard to violence, we are by nature an aggressive species with a history of physical and psychic violence. Killing is violence; greed and verbal abuse are also violence. Violence has many forms existing along a continuum from obvious to subtle, but at its base, violence is the destruction of well-being. The capacity for violence is built into our species through aggressive instincts related to survival. When that violence is unnecessary and avoidable, it is sin.

Under a traditional "rebellion against God" concept, it would be unthinkable to point to aggression, with its easy entailment of violence, as a cause of sin. A tendency toward aggression is built into human nature, so that if this tendency is a cause of sin, then the creator of human nature would be implicated in the fact of human sin. Hence the only creaturely basis of sin that could save the creator from implication was human freedom, for which each human was solely responsible. Since the universal misuse of freedom belied freedom's reality, the original sin of Adam accounted for the distorted conditions of freedom that lead all humans into sin. Thus human responsibility was preserved, and God the creator was kept free from culpability.

But a relational conceptuality posits a situation where the world is creation in a threefold sense, rather than in a unilateral sense. Under a supposition of God as unilateral creator, the cause of sin cannot be located in the finite situation per se. If it were, then God would share the guilt—and perhaps even the greater guilt—for God is presumably unconditioned by any necessity and acts out of the divine freedom and fully in accord with the divine nature. This impossible possibility of the guilt of God was rejected in the Christian tradition not by considering a more complex notion of creation, but by assigning all responsibility for sin to the free will of the creature. There could be nothing in nature itself that predisposes the creature toward sin.

But does the same objection hold if God and the world together share in the creation of the world? Earlier, I argued that every entity in the universe is creation in a three-fold sense: It is created by its past, since the past lays down the parameters to which it must in some way conform; the past emits the energy fields from which the new entity emerges. But every entity is also created by its future, mediated to it by God. God, acting out of a fullness of knowledge of the becoming creature's context, and also out of the effect of

God's own nature upon that context, offers the becoming creature its best creative possibility for unification of its past world. The third sense in which the world is creation is through each entity's response to past and future. In every standpoint of existence the becoming element of the world integrates its responsive feelings of its past and future; the "how" of this integration finally rests with the entity in question. Thus God is creator of the world *with* the world, overturning the long tradition of creation by divine fiat alone. All three factors—God, the past, and the subject—must be taken into consideration in order to understand the world as creation.

But in this case, one is no longer left with the onerous problem that if there is actually a finite inclination toward sin it must somehow be God the creator's fault. And, if some degree of freedom on a continuum from indeterminism toward at least our own degree of freedom is characteristic of every particle in the world, then creaturely freedom per se, and not simply human freedom, accounts in part for the way the world is. Therefore, if there are factors within the way the world is even prior to the emergence of human beings that can account for the universality of human perversity, then God is not necessarily the one to be held responsible for these factors. Rather, there is a shared responsibility between God and the world.

Creation is a process that takes place between God and the world, apparently unfolding and turning in on itself and moving yet again in an infinite number of ways. Whether the intricate process can be called "story" and treated as directional at all is certainly questionable; the most that can be said is that from our perspective of experienced beginnings and endings, we humans at least turn creation into story, into history.

We understand ourselves as coming into existence through a long process; our story emerges from artifacts our ancestors left behind. And if our creation spans a long period of time, and if God is ever a creative God, then are we not still in the process of our creation? What reason have we to think that we as a race are a "finished product," particularly given the raw cruelty to which we are prone? Perhaps our very incompletion in relation to the criterion of well-being is witness to the continual call of God, luring us toward our further creation.

Two theologians and two scientists offer guidance. Of the theologians, the first is Irenaeus, who pictured life as a schoolhouse of soulmaking where one might learn to become fully human, mirroring the very likeness of God. The second is Friedrich Schleier-macher, who developed a major theological understanding of the universality of sin through his understanding of evolution. The scientists are Christoph Wasserman, physicist and student of archaeological research, and the second is Irenaeus Eibl-Eibesfeldt, an ethologist whose studies focus on instinctive behavior in animals and human beings. Building on these thinkers, I suggest that innate human aggressiveness and its corollary violence are the basis for sin, and that God's continuing creative call is toward a transcendence of unnecessary violence. We are called toward a spirituality that embraces the well-being of all things. In such a process, aggressiveness itself may be dissociated from violence, and turned to an instrument for good.

Irenaeus wrote several centuries prior to Augustine, and therefore before the doctrine of original sin received its definitive form. As was noted in chapter one, a heuristic aspect to the doctrine of original sin was its ability to explain the pervasiveness of suffering as well as of sin, for all suffering—indeed, all evil—was considered to be the result of sin and its punishment. Irenaeus also attempted to account for the universality of sin and suffering, but he did so by considering the human race as a whole to be in its infancy. He made a distinction between creation in the image and creation in the likeness of God, with the former being the precondition of the latter. To be in the image of God was to be created with the capacity to become the likeness of God, but such likeness involved a necessarily painful process of learning. Life as we know it is precisely this process. But since the human creature is not yet so far advanced, and since in fact its ignorance involves it in sins that hinder it yet further, the Creator sent the Teacher, Christ, both to heal us from our sins and to show us the shining likeness of God. Through this healing and this empowering model, we are graciously enabled to live in love, which is the very likeness of God. This brief account of his complex understanding serves to show that a model of sin that draws upon the long emergence of the race is not entirely novel within the Christian tradition, since it bears some analogy to the thesis developed very early in Christian history by Irenaeus.

Friedrich Schleiermacher's nineteenth century development of the human condition in *The Christian Faith* offers a complementary thesis that the physical aspects of our existence preceded and provided the basis for spirituality. He posits that in the long evolution of humanity, our physicality involved a necessary self-preservation instinct that led to protection of one's own self or kind over against that which was defined as other. This mode of self-centeredness served well to insure the survival of the evolving human creature, much as it still serves the animal realm. But like Irenaeus, Schleiermacher saw our physical beginnings as existing for the sake of that which could emerge from physical existence, which is to say, the God-consciousness of spirituality.

For a creature to emerge with the capacity for a consciousness of God radically changes the nature of the world, and in fact allows it to "be" world as a place of meaning rather than simply earth apart from interpretation. Without such a creature, the earth is an interdependent network of many kinds and species of existences, but there is no single species with the ability to bring that interdependence to recognition. Without such recognition, the earth is not yet world—it is factually integrated, but not meaningfully integrated. In other words, apart from such a species, earth has no possibility of becoming world, and hence earth is not yet complete. The emergence of such a species is the transformation of "earth" into the human construct of "world." As such, earth is given a new unity in consciousness and in acts appropriate to that consciousness.

This world-as-one consciousness, however, depends upon a God-consciousness. One sees the earth as interdependent only through seeing the sense in which the self is thoroughly dependent upon God, and extending this knowledge to awareness that every element in the world is likewise thoroughly dependent upon God. But if all are God-dependent, then all are interconnected through this same God-dependence. The God-consciousness, then, is the means whereby the human species knows the interdependence of the world.

Knowing the world as interdependent involves the corollary of acting in terms of this interdependence. One's actions and one's knowledge are to be in conformity with the reality that all things exist interdependently, and together depend on the creative power of God. The center of one's existence shifts from a mode of survival of the self and one's own kind to a God-conscious mode. In this mode, one's concern and actions broaden to include the well-being of the whole in relation to God. This is what Schleiermacher called the God-consciousness, or spirituality, and it is the completion of creation.

The problem, of course, is that spirituality must emerge as a novelty in the world, based in physicality, but transcending physicality. The very fact that God-consciousness can emerge follows from the effectiveness of the preceding self-centeredness of physicality. Self-centeredness has yielded the survival and growth of the species into a complexity that can now support its own transcendence. In order to achieve that transcendence, however, self-centeredness must be released, replaced by the God-consciousness of recognized interdependence. Thus the emergent spirituality struggles against the basis for its existence, and is called upon to reverse the very orientation that allowed its emergence. Schleiermacher names the attendant tension as the basis for sin and for evil.

In the nature of the case, humans must sin. The emergence of the God-consciousness is at once the judgment upon a self-centered mode of survival. One's freedom is first exercised in knowing oneself a sinner. Self-judgment is the nascent God-consciousness, emerging through the process of discovering itself to be caught in sin. This act of self-judgment is an act of freedom and responsibility. Only through freedom can one discover oneself to be a sinner. All would be well if such a discovery allowed a clear break with sin, so that henceforth one only acted for the sake of the interrelational whole in the name of God. Unfortunately, this eludes human achievement. The human predicament is that the nascent spirituality is much weaker than the long-established self-centeredness. Further, the interconnectedness of all means that one's own self-centeredness is reinforced by that of many others, making the problem of extrication that much more difficult. For Schleiermacher, this precedence of the physical nature and subsequent difficulty of the emerging spiritual nature functioned in the role of original sin.

Schleiermacher resolved the problem of original sin by God's own interjection into creation through incarnation in the form of The Redeemer. The Redeemer, being of God, is capable of that which the rest of humanity so sorely fails. But being also of humanity, The Redeemer fits into the interconnectedness of all finite existence, so that what The Redeemer accomplishes becomes a fact of existence that affects all. And The Redeemer, who is God incarnate in Jesus of Nazareth, lives a perfect God-consciousness, proclaims that consciousness, and establishes a community that like leaven in a loaf will eventually mediate that God-consciousness to the rest of humanity. In The Redeemer, the world achieves its completion, and humanity achieves its release from its imprisoning sin.

Although twentieth century philosophers and theologians have dealt with evolutionary theories,[1] one would be hard pressed to say that the notions of sin or violence were major interests within these developments. Rather, two scientists of philosophical bent contribute material from which to build upon Schleiermacher's connection between sin and evolution. Christoph Wassermann, in an essay called "The Evolutionary Understanding of Man and the Problem of Evil,"[2] works from the concrete results of archaeological research. He notes four major transitions in the evolution of humankind, seeing in each transition a double-edged consequence holding new forms of good and evil. He begins with that period of prehistory dated approximately three million years ago when two types of hominids appear to have existed on the African continent. The larger was purely vegetarian, while the smaller form was meat-eating. Evidence indicates that the vegetarian species did not survive changing ecological conditions of the successive droughts that occurred during the last stages of the Pliocene era and into the early stages of the Pleistocene period. The hunters, however, survived. The mobility of a nomadic hunting existence allowed this species to move with the game, and so survive the droughts. But the survival was purchased in large part through the violent death of wild animals and hominids not belonging to the local kin group.[3]

Wassermann traces a tendency toward culture activities that slowly emerged, most notably through the transition to chopping stones into tools that occurred over a period in the lower Pleistocene era. This was the period of "hunting and gathering" societies, and their emergence was largely, though not entirely, connected with an evolving efficiency in accomplishing the violent deaths upon which the species depended for its food. At the same time, however, tool-

---

[1] For example, S. Alexander in *Space Time and Deity* (New York: Macmillan, 1950); Alfred North Whitehead in *Adventures of Ideas* (New York: The Free Press, 1967); Teilhard de Chardin, *The Phenomenon of Man* (New York: Harper & Row, 1959) all presuppose an evolutionary structure to the universe, with the general movement of the universe related in various ways to the intensification of deity. While each author deals with evil in relation to this teleology, none develops a physiological basis for sin comparable to Schleiermacher.

[2] Christoph Wassermann, "The Evolutionary Understanding of Man and the Problem of Evil," published in: H. May, ed., *Kooperation und Wettbewerb: Zur Ethik und Biologie menschlichen Sozialverhaltens* (Loccumer Protokolle Bd. 75, 1989). Also published in C. Wassermann, *Struktur und Ereignis: Interdisziplinaere Studien in Physik, Theologie und Philosophie* (Genf: Faculté Autonome de Théologie Protestant, 1991). Wasserman draws heavily from the works of C. S. Chard and K. F. Weaver in developing his theories.

[3] Ibid., p. 293

making also marked an advance toward greater complexity of existence and greater possibilities for stability of existence.

The transition to the Neolithic age involved the development of farming and the domestication of animals, with the dramatic result that human beings began to control their environment. Wassermann points out that as animals became domesticated, the human entered into a fundamentally different relationship with other species. Previously, the relationship to animals was one of inflicting violent death—or of encountering one's own violent death in the struggle. With domestication, the human still killed the animal, but only after a period of sustaining the animal. Meanwhile, as plants were also domesticated a means was found—nearly two million years following the first vegetarian hominids—of sustaining life apart from the violent killing of other life. With regard to non-kinship groups, slavery became an alternative response to killing, so that a way was found to incorporate the stranger within the kin group. With the changing fortunes of generations, groups initially enslaved evolved into partners, creating greater diversity within a single society.

Wassermann next examines the introduction of urbanism to human life, and its evidently new behavioral patterns of codes of law and warfare. As geographical proximity replaced kinship as the common factor in group life, laws were necessary for the limitation of intragroup violence, subverting the endless chain of retribution for perceived wrongs. But laws then as now could be used for social oppression as well as for security. The invention of wheeled vehicles and forms of metal for the sake of more power in warfare also had repercussions for more complex forms of cultural life. Thus once again, the increase in the human ability to inflict violent death was integrally related to the human ability to evolve more complex forms of social life.

Wassermann develops the thesis that human survival necessarily entailed violence, but that the violence itself was ambiguous, yielding life-enhancing as well as life-destroying behavior. Irenaeus Eibl-Eibesfeldt develops a similar thesis, but from a contemporary study of animal and human behavior.[4] He argues that living creatures possess instincts toward aggression and instincts toward social bonding. The first yields violence, whether toward those beyond or within

---

[4] Irenaeus Eibl-Eibesfeldt, *Love and Hate* (New York: Holt, Rinehart and Winston, 1971).

the kin group, and he argues convincingly that there is no living species without violent behavior.[5] The second is a general drive within individuals to seek and maintain some form of closeness with another.

Eibl-Eibesfeldt carried out extensive studies on innate behavior patterns in birds and animals, showing conclusively that inherited motor patterns exist and become manifest, whether or not the creature has ever seen another of its kind. He also investigated human motor behavior through a great variety of cultures, documenting what appear to be universal responses to similar stimuli, such as meeting friends or strangers, and experiencing pleasure, fear, or pain. Furthermore, he documents the great similarity between humans and primates in their motor responses to such fundamental situations. Eventually his study takes us to instinctual responses of aggression that lead to violence, not only in animals, but also in humans. The universality of the responses indicates that the manner of response is coded within physiological structures of the species.

Animal aggression is related to survival through establishing territorial boundaries that protect a food supply, and through contests between rival males that insure that the stronger male will mate and participate in protecting the progeny. Turning to a discussion of human aggression, Eibl-Eibesfeldt notes the persistence of both types of aggression, albeit often in transmuted form. Human territorial instincts can be as innocuous as preferring to be the sole person using a library table, or as invidious as territorial wars. Mating rivalries are supplemented with a much wider diffusion of interwoven aggression and pleasure through ritual, games, and intellectual rivalries. In either case, physiological responses of aggression are remarkably similar across cultures, whether through facial expressions, clenching of fists, or the types of threatening displays that are employed.

Eibl-Eibesfeldt argues that when aggressive tendencies are aroused they build up physiological tensions that seek discharge through psychic or physical violence, and that this resolution to

---

[5] In response to critics who point to peaceful groups as proof that aggression and violence are not universal characteristics, Eibl-Eibesfeldt implicitly shows the androcentric bias of critics who judge peacefulness on the basis of man-to-man behavior, discounting the acceptability within some of these societies of male violence toward a wife. He also notes acceptable forms of violence within "peaceful" cultures toward objects and among children, and documents the ritualization of violence in all societies.

aggressive impulses can be a means of pleasure. Human society has evolved ritualistic modes for dealing safely with aggressive impulses, such as contests and other methods of social control. The methods vary from culture to culture—but Eibl-Eibesfeldt argues that in no culture do these methods eliminate the violence of aggression, and in fact the methods can stimulate the very violence they are intended to control. For example, violent films in western culture provide a cathartic outlet for aggression. However, the stimuli of the films also arouse aggressive instincts within the viewer. Insofar as the violence is resolved within the film, the viewer also experiences release, but if the plot does not provide resolution sufficient to the tension created, the tension will be released elsewhere. Social controls for dealing with aggression thus can contribute to the very problem they supposedly address.

The force of Eibl-Eibesfeldt's work is his demonstration of the universality and physiological basis of aggressive instincts in human life, and the strong implication that these instincts derive from our own evolutionary history. If his work stopped there, he might arguably make a case for despair, for violence then is inescapably entwined with who we are and who we can be. But his argument goes further, showing that there is also an innate basis for human bonding, again developing the similarities with the primates and the universality of human behavior patterns. Much as Freud saw the pleasure principle and the death principle as existing in tension, even so Eibl-Eibesfeldt argues for a tension between aggression and bonding, building upon it his hope that the instinct toward bonding might increasingly be the antidote that controls the more destructive instinct of aggression.

By drawing from all four of these thinkers, we can connect the religious and secular analysis of violence in relation to evolution. From Irenaeus we note the deep roots within the Christian tradition of the theory that human creation is a long process in which we are still involved. Schleiermacher's modern form of this sensitivity suggests that physicality precedes spirituality, and is its necessary foundation. Wassermann carries the evolutionary theory further through the archaeological evidence suggesting that our long physical struggle depended integrally, if ambiguously, on the fact of human violence, and Eibl-Eibesfeldt gives a descriptive analysis of the contemporary phenomenon of aggression throughout life. Thus the analysis of aggression and violence of these two twentieth century thinkers provides a more empirical grounding to the intuitions of Irenaeus and Schleiermacher concerning the role of sin in the evolving history of the human race.

One implication of the work of Wasserman and Eibl-Eibesfeldt requires a curious modification in Augustine's dependence upon a first human pair as responsible for the fact that all humans, throughout all generations, sin. Twentieth century theologians such as Reinhold Niebuhr, as noted earlier, use this "pair" as a metaphor for the psychological structure of the human being. In many ways, "anxiety" equals "Adam." But if one factors the long and violent evolution of the human species into theological thinking, then the "first pair" is transmuted into the "first million (or more) years" that account for the transition from hominid to human existence. As a species we present human beings all wear the mark of Cain, not on our foreheads, but within our souls. We have evolved through a long history of violent death, and retain a continued penchant to inflict violence on life. Our birthmark is a common capacity for violence, or an aggressiveness written deep within the structures of our being. This heritage lies behind our universal ability to live and act in such a way that we violate the well-being of some aspect of creation. We sin.

Schleiermacher argued that without spirituality, there is no sin. My claim is that without the ability to transcend our violent tendency, there may be evil, but it is not yet sin. The supposition is that in the emergence of the human race there came a period when the species was capable of sustaining a degree of self-transcendence.[6] I posit that the "breath of life" whereby the hominid became human occurred at that point where the creature was able to transcend immersion in self-identity by empathic recognition of other-identity. The ability to empathize with the other as other is at the same time the ability to imagine, even if only the ability to imagine the subjectivity of the other. One might speculate that the art forms on the walls of caves indicate the emergence of such transcendence, but in the nature of the case so fragile an experience, unlike the chopping of stones into weapons, leaves little trace for later generations to discover. How does one record the birth of spirit, or the discovery of the subjectivity of the other, and therefore of oneself?

---

[6] Eibl-Eibesfeldt's analysis of an instinct for social bonding that parallels the instinct for aggression is helpful, but not yet sufficient. Apart from some form of transcendence, one simply follows one's instincts, whether toward violence or toward bonding. What is required is the ability to temper the one with the other, and this can only be done through some form of transcendence.

Even so, the discovery of relation through empathy, memory, and imagination, and the needless violation of relation, is the beginning identity of humankind as "sinner." For the presence of that transcendence in any degree meant that it was possible to do otherwise.

Schleiermacher's model again illumines us. Almost by definition, spirituality involves the human creature in sin. The same must be said when the terms "survival through violence" and "transcendence through empathy, memory, and imagination" are used. The issue is that the very awareness that one can do otherwise can only take place in the parallel awareness that hitherto one had *not* done otherwise. Prior to transcendence, the acts of violence were done under the instinct of necessity, or one might say innocence. But with the first knowledge that one could do otherwise comes the retrospective knowledge that one had not done otherwise, which means that the past becomes perceived through the new-found knowledge of sin.

The condition of original sin, then, involves aggressive tendencies within our humanity that naturally incline us toward violence. Instincts toward bonding are also primal within us, and self-transcendence through memory, empathy, and imagination makes it possible for bonding rather than aggressiveness to be our dominant mode of being. To the extent that we do not avoid unnecessary violence, we live in sin. To this day, we continue to deal with aggressive tendencies toward violence as the stuff from which our sin is fashioned.

Traditional Christian doctrine has certainly recognized the violence of humankind, but has maintained that first came pride, which was then the cause of violence. This theory suggests that violence came first, which then became the cause of pride as the self-construed justification of violence. Traditional theology still defines pride as the undue exaltation of the self, or the attempt to establish one's own borders, independently of considerations of the good of others. Most typically, these borders were construed psychically rather than physically, as is evident in the classic theme adopted by Christianity of the "overreacher."[7] But the studies above suggest that innate aggression rather than pride leads to the violent defiance of

---

[7] Perhaps the most dominant image in literature of the "overreacher" is Faust, who refuses to accept the limitations of creatureliness. Pride as the overreaching of one's boundaries went beyond geographic territory (which Christian nations often felt called of God to violate), and generally referred to boundaries of creatureliness or culturally defined roles.

boundaries, and that psychic forms of this violence are transmuta-
tions of the more fundamental physical forms related to aggressive
territorialism. Thus aggression and violence do not emerge from
pride; pride emerges from aggression and its attendant violence.

Pride emerges from aggression as a way of dealing with the tension created by the violation of one's own ability to transcend violence. Violence is disregard of the well-being of the other. When
this takes place in the context of transcendence, then a tension is
created in the self-understanding, for transcendence relates one
empathically to the violated other. How is such a tension resolved?
The most common way is a deceptive denial of relationship, which
of course entails the denial of the empathic regard for the other as
subject. One continues in the primitive mode of regarding the other
as object, thus searing the transcendent knowledge sufficiently to
allow the violence to continue. One justifies one's continuing actions
of violation by assuming the right to such violation. In short, violation engenders a sinful mode of pride as a way of coping with
the transcendent consciousness that whispers the knowledge of sin.
Through the means of pride, one dulls the very essence of one's
humanity—which means, of course, that if pride pretends an exaltation, it does so paradoxically from an actual lessening of the fullness
of what it can mean to be human.

This sinful mode of pride is to be sharply distinguished from the
holy and healthy strength of ego that facilitates the openness of the
self to the other. This, too, is pride in the form of a relationally
based esteem of self, and it can well be a means of manifesting truth,
love, and beauty. Such pride recognizes the truth of the relational
interdependence of the self with all others; it participates in love
toward mutual well-being in relationship, and this togetherness of
truth and love inexorably weaves the world into yet a new form of
beauty. The undue self-exaltation of sinful pride is a perversion
of the self-and-other exultation of a reality-based relational pride
that is fostered through the esteem of the relational self.

A variation on the tradition's focus on pride as the original and
besetting sin is self-centeredness, which we have already seen in its
use by Schleiermacher. But self-centeredness as well as pride can
be seen as emerging from violence. Intensified transcendence is the
persistent call of the creator God to move beyond violence. Self-
centeredness is the refusal to move beyond instinctive violence in
the many modes we have devised for its expression. It is to stay
in the trajectory of violence, whether in its physical or psychic

modes of expression, and never fully to open oneself to the full humanity to which God calls us. Paradoxically, of course, such "self-centeredness" is really the loss of the self, and a stunted humanity, since the fullness of the self requires the openness to relation that empathy and imagination make possible. It is not a loss of transcendence, for this is not possible; it is the minimization of transcendence in favor of the long established trajectory of violence. Since this mode of self-centeredness requires an essential passivity, its expression most often tends toward the psychic rather than physical modes of violence. In this sense it is the other side of pride, which more typically expresses its denial of transcendence through active aggrandizement of others.

The tradition also pointed to "unbelief" as the essence of all sin, claiming that the condition of failing to rely upon the promises of God results in a failure to love God or others. This interpretation presupposes the need to earn one's eternal salvation through proper loving, whether this be done personally or vicariously as the gift of God. No mere human being fulfills this condition, which led the church fathers to argue that all wills were defective because of original sin. And this original sin was projected as Adam's failure to rely upon God, which was both unbelief and pride. As a result, one now loves others in order to qualify for one's own salvation, in which case what appears to be love is really manipulation of others toward one's own good.

This construal of the human situation is somewhat problematic for several reasons from a process-relational viewpoint. Since the well-being of the self is inextricably related to the well-being of the other, there is no clear distinction between loving oneself and loving another. To make such a distinction fundamental to one's world-view brings that view into question.

To be sure, some process theologians, as was noted in chapter three, have argued that deviation from God's initial aim constitutes the basic issue of sin. But there I argued that God's aims are necessarily deeper than conscious levels of the self. Therefore, one's mode of response to these aims is not an intentional response to God's own self, but is rather a response to the subject matter of that aim. Hence "unbelief" becomes a strained way of interpreting a failure to conform oneself to God-given possibilities.

If belief is interpreted as a non-conscious disposition of the self, then a corollary can be made between sin as unbelief and sin as deviation from God's initial aims. "Faith" is then a better word than "belief," since faith can denote one's orientation toward life in a way that is affected by, but deeper than, one's particular belief in or about God.

But what of that other notion of the predisposing condition of sin, anxiety? Some might argue that anxiety is the cause of violence, but the historical fact would seem to reverse that assumption. Before we emerged as humanity, the hominid from which we came was surviving precisely through violent killing. If the transition to humanity—or, in Schleiermacher's terms, spirituality—has something to do with transcendence, then anxiety as Niebuhr and others describe it is not present until that transcendence is present. Hence historically, violence precedes anxiety, and in fact produces anxiety.

One further mode of response to the call of transcendence is to use the call as a way of extending the forms of violence beyond the physical and into the spiritual sphere. Usually there is no sharp differentiation between the two forms, which is to say that where there is physical violence there is also psychic violence, such as in sexism, racism, and the many similar modes of oppression. The psychic forms are the stereotyping that tends to demean the self-image of the other and restrict self-development possibilities for the other, and therefore, of course, to rob of the other's future. Psychic forms of violence are particularly related to the refusal of self-transcendence through empathy and imagination, but they are refusals of these gifts through distortion rather than through outright rejection. For example, it takes imagination and sadism, which is a distortion of empathy, to envision the suffering caused to another by symbolically putting that other on a cross and setting that cross ablaze with the fires of hell within burning distance of a home.

The Amnesty International account of violence toward children illustrates the bent toward violence named as the primal sin in this chapter, but it also shows the horror when aggressive tendencies are exercised through the capacity for transcendence. Two of the cases specifically involved extended torture of children. If aggression forms a substratum of our human nature, can this alone account for the sadistic brutality involved in deliberately causing extensive pain to defenseless children? Apparently it is possible so to repress one's capacity for empathy that the bent toward violence plus a position of power combine not only to unleash violence, but to wed it to imaginative power so as to devise uglier and more devastating acts of violence. Violence without imagination acts quickly; violence with imagination is demonically slow. Aggression and violence apart from transcendence may be evil, but they are not yet sin; aggression and violence exercised within the capacity for self-transcendence distort those capacities by extending the range of violence.

And so our original dynamics as a violent species have not seemed to abate in the short period of our evolution. Insofar as we have used the very means given to transcend our violence as further instruments of violence, we have intensified our problems. Violent killing emerged with the human species as a way of survival. But we have survived, and now through the extension of the very violence that brought us to prominence on this earth, we threaten to destroy not only each other, and whole species of other animal life, but even the planet itself. Anxiety emerges as a relationally based response to the pervasive effects of violence throughout the earth. Pride and self-centeredness are ways of coping with and covering our own sins of needless violence. They well serve the suppression of that transcendent call of God to turn from unnecessary violence as a mode of survival. But they ill serve the need and hope that we might yet embrace the glory that is this earth with intents and actions toward well-being. Instead, we continue to be prey to our own violence, the sin that so easily besets us.

SIN

The government already has written off $270 million that it was supposed to charge polluters for cleanup of the nation's worst toxic waste sites and faces absorbing hundreds of millions more, an Associated Press review has found.

The Environmental Protection Agency says in many cases the polluters have disappeared or are unable to pay.

—*Bangor Daily News*
Monday, June 21, 1993

6

SIN THROUGH HUMAN SOLIDARITY

The tendency to violence that persists in human nature is the ground of sin. The evolutionary emergence of transcendence in the modes of memory, empathy, and imagination marks the transition to actual sin, which is needless violence against any aspect of creation. Such violence is the working of ill-being and constitutes rebellion against creation's good. To all appearances, all humans sin.

This universal participation in sin rests not only in our bent toward violence, but also in our solidarity with the human race. We are individuals, but we are also participants in an organic whole much greater than ourselves, the human species. In an interrelated world, all things co-exist, and those things most closely related to ourselves in the vast scheme of things exercise a definitive impact on who we are and how we are. Through the organic solidarity of the race, we are affected by the sins of others, and our own sins likewise have an effect upon all others.

With regard to the immediate participants in sin, the effect is usually a quite conscious lessening of one's well-being. But the corollary ill-being is not limited to the immediate participants. Through the solidarity of the race, it is subliminally mediated to all. And I will argue that a responsive anxiety is the half-way house between non-conscious and conscious experience of sin as mediated through the solidarity of the race. Existential anxiety, contra Tillich and Niebuhr, is not based in human finitude, but in the direct and indirect experience of violence. And indirect violence is mediated through the interconnected solidarity of our species.

I know of no keener expression of human solidarity than that

achieved by Fyodor Dostoyevsky in *The Brothers Karamazov*.
Throughout the book, he contrasts two forms of relation: That
of the objective observer of the world, and that of the subjective
participant in the world. In one sense, the course of this complex
novel is the story of the tension between these two ways of relating
to the world, and the gradual triumph of the subjective over the
objective.

Ivan Karamazov and his sinister shadow, Rakitin, represent the
rationally objective response to the world, and Alyosha Karamazov
and the monk Zossima represent a compassionately subjective response. In both cases, Rakitin and Zossima are idealized forms of
the objectivity and subjectivity they respectively represent, whereas
the brothers Ivan and Alyosha more ambiguously portray these
positions.

By degrees, the once distant Ivan, who first speaks of evil as that
which he has learned at arms' length from newspaper reports, dis-
covers his own inextricable participation in evil. Finally he realizes
himself to be at the very center of that evil. Since reason had been
his mode of distancing himself from evil, he loses his reason in the
madness of discovering his complicity. Having relied so fully upon
his ability to achieve distance, he cannot make the transition to compassionate participation that would redeem him within the world,
and so save his sanity, his self, and his brother Dmitri who is falsely
condemned for parricide. Ivan's dissolution comes about despite
the contrary example he has in his brother Alyosha, who through
compassion survives his own participation in evil.

The saving subjective response to the world—and what I have
called the transcendence of empathy—is epitomized by the monk
Zossima, as well as Alyosha, his disciple. Zossima, like Ivan, has
undergone a transition from observer to unwitting participant in
evil. Zossima, like Ivan, also had a brother who empathically recognized his relational identification with all. At Zossima's nadir point
of knowing his complicity in evil, his own brother's example influenced his conversion to compassionate love for all existing persons
and things. For Zossima, nothing human is alien to him; all, like
him, are involved in evil to varying degrees; all, like him, yearn for
goodness to varying degrees. This discovery of subjective solidarity
is not abstract—for that would be the "love of humanity" that exalts
humanity as an idea and despises actual human beings. Rather,
solidarity is the recognition of one's connectedness to all others.
Through this connectedness comes one's own participation in every

evil, and with it, a share in the responsibility for all evil. However, in a manner reminiscent of Schleiermacher's understanding of the effectiveness of The Redeemer, one's connectedness also becomes the means whereby redeeming love—for love always redeems—is mediated to all. The solidarity of the race is the means of mediating sin and also the means of mediating compassionate love.

Alyosha knows himself from the beginning of the novel to be a participant in evil as well as good, but he shows himself more clearly than Zossima to be personally involved in both. That is, while his bent is toward the good, he ever recognizes his tainted "Karamazov blood." His own complicity in the central evil of parricide is to block out his sensitivities to the progress of the tragedy, ultimately sleeping through the actual crime. Through this he demonstrates the perversion of empathy into the idealized "love of humanity" in abstraction rather than through attentive involvement. Love, to be love, must be conditioned by the truthful seeing of that which is loved. To love is to discern the true condition of the other. Alyosha's own movement toward a true empathy is his transition from a somewhat sentimental identification with all, that is in its own way as separate as Ivan's objectivity, to his entering into the challenging engagement of empathic love. This takes place as he enters fully into the experience of his brothers, and by extension through his somewhat eschatological relation to the schoolboys in the latter part of the novel.

Dostoyevsky inextricably joins violence with concupiscence in the raw and cunning sensuous nature of the father, Fyodor Karamazov. Like the sons of Adam, the brothers born from this nature carry its effects within themselves as the taint of inherited sin. Parricide deals with this inheritance by violence, using violence to destroy violence.[1] But this is no resolution: the violence is underlined, escalated, and perpetuated rather than eliminated. Dostoyevsky eschews such a response in favor of exalting the solidarity of the race achieved by compassionate subjectivity. This is the awareness of the interconnected oneness of all humanity, and the concomitant response of human life lived through compassionate love.

The Brothers Karamazov provides me with a profound literary illus-

---

[1] Sigmund Freud and Rene Girard might each, in their own way, see the killing of the father as a recapitulation of the primal crime. The function of the parricide within the novel, however, is to reveal the complicity of all four brothers in evil. None are innocent, whether through the intellectualism of Ivan, the saintliness of Alyosha, the impetuous sensuality of Dmitri, or the madness and abuse of Smerdyakov.

tration of the solidarity of the race and the effect of this solidarity for the universality of sin. Relational theology attempts to delineate the underlying nature of the world that yields such solidarity. This has already been discussed to a large extent in earlier chapters: Each reality receives from all that have preceded it, and gives to all who succeed it. This receiving and giving is a dynamic transition of energy, drawn into the interiority of each existing thing. Thus relationships are not secondary characteristics of things; rather, in and through relationships each thing becomes itself. Relationships are constitutive of existence, and therefore through relationships all things are woven together. Evil anywhere is mediated everywhere through the relational structure of existence.

Nature provides an illustration of this transmission of quality from one thing to another through the lowly alder tree often found in wetlands. The alder is not an especially attractive tree; spindly and mottled, it shoots its branches into the air in a way that is half bush-like and half tree-like. But the homely alder is actually a great gift to other trees in its vicinity. This tree is capable not only of absorbing nitrogen from the soil for its own use, but through its root system the tree transfers nitrogen to other trees in its area, whether or not they are directly contiguous with the alder. What is done here, in the alder, has an effect there, on the white spruce: the spruce, receiving the nitrogen from the alder, is stronger and healthier than it would be on its own.

Even so, the internal nature of relationships means that what happens in one entity has an effect on all entities. When this effect is evil, that evil spreads until it touches all. It seeps pervasively through the ground, percolating from depths of original sin and personalized sin in ever-successive layers of pollution. And the effects are not simply external, like a stain that can be washed away. Rather, the effects are internalized within each affected entity, forming one aspect of how the entity experiences the world. The interrelationality of existence creates a solidarity of the race that involves each in the plight of all.

If Dostoyevsky illustrates this interrelationality in a positive way, the news account heading this chapter illustrates interrelationality in a negative way. For the sake of increasing profits, corporations persisted in operations whose side effects included the production of contaminants that could not be safely contained. These toxic substances were then disposed of in selected sites, where they seeped into the land and/or water, negatively affecting the land, the water, and living beings.

The social answer to the problem was to charge the polluter for the cost of cleaning the environment, and in some cases, companies honored this obligation and attempted to redress the ill-being they caused. But the Associated Press reports that "hundreds of millions" of dollars are not forthcoming from the polluters. The clean-up funds, then, must be absorbed by the nation as a whole.

Insofar as the clean-up costs are provided by the taxpayers, it is quite obvious how the sins of some become the burden of all. But the deeper message is that the burden is not simply financial, it is medical and ecological. Pollution violates the well-being of earth and its inhabitants, creating disease and dis-ease both consciously and subliminally. The effects are mediated throughout the nation and throughout the earth. The financial impact recorded in the article is surpassed by the physical and psychic impact.

The singularly important facet of relational reality is that the old views of the solidarity of the race have a basis in ontic fact. Whether we like it or not, we are bound up with one another's good, woven into one another's welfare. Such a reality is easy to acknowledge at the personal level, but the deeper reality is that our relationality extends far wider than our consciousness is capable of handling. To live in a relational universe is to be affected physically and psychically by everything and everyone that exists. We are bound up with one another throughout the earth, inexorably inheriting from each, inexorably influencing all. Our prized individuality exists through connectedness.

Through connectedness, every act of violence reverberates throughout the race. Like Ivan, I use newspaper accounts to illustrate the concrete nature of sin, but like Alyosha, I intend these accounts to illustrate in an extraordinary way what is, after all, the ordinary world of us all, deeply affecting each one of us in the core of our being. And while the type of violence news reports consider "newsworthy" are the egregious cases I am citing, this is not to underestimate the pain and ill-being caused by the more humble modes of violence of everyday relationships. Common greed, intentional undercutting of another's esteem, lying, and manipulation are among the more "polite" modes of violence that weave themselves in and around daily life as the raw violence of physical injury becomes domesticated into the subtle violence of social intercourse. Whether subtle or raw, each act of violence spreads throughout the whole race, conditioning what and how each member of the race can be. We are each participants in every act of violence, whether or not we are aware of these acts.

Relationships do not depend upon consciousness in order to be effective. Indeed, most relationships are much deeper than consciousness, and our finite minds are not equipped to bring this massive detail into awareness. The very organization of our bodies seems to include something like very efficient and complex "screening devices" that sift and narrow the data with which we deal, so that only a minute portion reaches the level that we call consciousness. Our sensory system, for example, not only mediates data to us, it also deflects data. We see only so many colors on the spectrum—but we are affected even by those rays that we cannot see. As information is channeled to and through our brains, most information stays at subliminal levels, handled unconsciously by our autonomic nervous system. Consciousness itself is also a complex mediating device, dealing with far more data at pre-or subconscious levels than what finally emerges in that tiny realm we name consciousness. Thus the enormous amount of energy, influence, and data mediated to us through relational existence is carefully winnowed and channeled through the complexity that is ourselves. But whether relations make it to consciousness or not, we are affected and we respond, inexorably, to all of them.

We are internally and directly related to every element in our past actual world. The implication, of course, is that the relationality that makes up the personal world of each one of us encompasses all other persons, as well as all elements in the universe preceding us. Insofar as violence takes place anywhere, it is mediated in varying degrees to all. Usually most of this internalization of violence remains at subliminal levels, outside of our consciousness. The more directly involved in violence we are, the more violence invades our consciousness. We experience the full force of the ill-being of sin.

There are two basic aspects of the experience of sin through solidarity to be developed before moving on to the discussion of the third level of original sin, social inheritance. The first aspect has to do with the existential impact of being involved in violence through solidarity, apart from consciousness. One could well raise the question, if one is not conscious of the violence, then what difference does it make? Could one not in effect live an anaesthetized life, avoiding the interrelational violence as much as possible so long as it isn't direct? And the second aspect follows from this, and has to do with the modes of response that are open relative to the existential violence inherent in solidarity.

The first issue forces us to look again at Niebuhr and Tillich in their analysis of anxiety as the precondition for sin. Both spoke of an existential anxiety, and related it to the tenuousness of life, so that one's finitude and mortality became the presenting reasons for the anxiety that lies just behind the door of our consciousness. But looking at the implications of interrelational existence with regard to violence suggests a different reading.

I have already argued that mortality alone is not the pervasive problem of existence. More often than not, elderly persons express a readiness to die, and persons experiencing great pain often long for death. In the complex busyness of daily life, most persons in good health are far more likely to be concerned with immediate and long range tasks and relationships than with thoughts of death. Children still seem to consider themselves immortal, and young adults are usually more concerned with birth than death. Throughout life, the intensity and fullness of living often leaves little time for concerns about dying. This is not necessarily an avoidance of death; it is far more direct than that. One simply has no time for death, till it happens. And when it inevitably does within one's intimate circles, even then our mourning soon becomes crowded out by the insistent demands of life.

Our failure to be preoccupied with death is not necessarily an avoidance of death and its attendant anxiety, but simply the fact that our anxiety over death is focused rather than pervasive. We become anxious about death with the discovery of a serious illness in ourselves or in others, or in situations of grave danger. But to claim that a pervasive existential anxiety is due to the eventual death of ourselves or our loved ones seems to go beyond the evidence. In short, while human death certainly can produce anxiety, in itself it is not sufficient to account for any pervasiveness of anxiety in human existence.

But if in fact we continuously absorb into our becoming all of the violence in the human world, and if we are also affected albeit to a lesser degree by all forms of violence anywhere, and if this subliminal experience of violence is intertwined with our most basic beginnings in every moment, then is it so farfetched to suggest that the subliminal experience of violence gives rise to an existential anxiety?

To live in a world where the most basic fact of existence is that life requires other life in order to live is to live in a world that is necessarily marked by violence. To be sure, we do not normally consider the act of eating to be an act of violence, but *what* we eat, whether animal or vegetable, loses its life to sustain ours. This mode of violence barely begins the forms of violence that pervade our human world. We participate in violence in many modes, at many levels, from economic deprivations of entire populations, to various psychic oppressions of many peoples, to the outright physical and mental agony inflicted upon persons through wars, political tortures, and crime. And if through the solidarity of the race we necessarily are affected by all violence everywhere, we must perforce respond to this violence, whether subliminally or consciously. And the subliminal response is simply anxiety.

Paul Tillich and Reinhold Niebuhr pinpointed a fundamental anxiety within human existence, and explained this anxiety as awareness of our finitude, of our being towards death. But a relational theology explains anxiety not by appealing to our death, but by pointing to the experience of violence mediated to us all through our interconnectedness. The solidarity of the human race is such that violence anywhere is experienced, however diluted, everywhere. Violence is like that distant drum relentlessly beating not quite beyond one's hearing, and its effect is dis-ease, anxiety.

One could speculate that the American obsession with guns and violence, whether for sport, for "protection," or for entertainment, is our attempt to channel our subliminal involvement with violence into the control of consciousness. We delude ourselves into believing that we can control the firing of our weapons, that we can confine our violence through channeling it into an arena or ring, and that we can turn the power of our televisions off, and so exercise control over the violence that we thus safely allow into our lives. But anxiety mocks our control, and can too often escape to become the devouring demon we fear. Violence, not death, is at the root of our anxieties, and our attempts to channel violence simply increase its ceaseless flow.

And while the power of violence certainly includes its ability to inflict death, the horror of violence is its ability to inflict prolonged pain, ill-being, and grief. Our conscious response takes the form of locking doors, buying insurance, and seeing to the availability of antidotes to anxiety. Thus the major effect of the pervasive if subliminal experience of violence through the solidarity of the race is the edge of anxiety with which we struggle.

I spoke earlier of the natural "sifting devices" that organize and coordinate the data of human experience. Given the great barrage of data affecting us at every moment, apart from some such ordering function within the human body and psyche we could have no organized experience at all. We would be overwhelmed with the magnitude of data. The capacity to negate data, or relegate it to irrelevance in our ongoing constitution, functions to keep the vast amount of violence in the world below our conscious experience. However, the emotive effect of this gatekeeping is anxiety. One can negate the data, but one cannot eliminate the feeling response to the data one has negated; hence anxiety arises.

Our existence as part of an interdependent world, where relations to all others are internal to the constitution of the self, creates a solidarity with the human race, and possibly with all species in descending degrees of intensity. We are, then, no matter how personally in control of our own violent tendencies, surrounded by and invaded by a vast amount of violence. We have relationally internalized these events, even though the vast majority of them, if not all, are certainly far below the level of conscious experience. Violence is the cause of anxiety, and the root of sin. It is mediated not simply through the bent to violence built into our humanity, but by an interrelational solidarity that mediates the effects of violence throughout the race.

But what are the responses to such a plight? If through solidarity we are affected by each and every act of violence; if through solidarity we affect each and every other being through our own acts of violence, are we then undone? As Dostoevsky illustrates, the responses to the experience of violence can either increase or ameliorate the levels of violence with which we continually deal.

One mode of responding to violence is simply to conform oneself to it. That is, violence threatens to overwhelm us, to consume us. When that violence is perceived as other to oneself, one way of dealing with the threat is to negate not the violence, but the "otherness" of violence. One can conform oneself to it, becoming it, and therefore no longer being the object of its attack. One gives up the self as "other" by blending it into the opposing force. This dynamic is operative in the formation of organized groups of violence, whether teen-age gangs or adult organized crime. But since the solidarity of the race means that the violence one inflicts must be subliminally taken back into oneself, conformity to violence through joining forces with violence cannot address the existential anxiety created through violence.

Conforming to violence also happens when one uses violence to fight violence. In such instances the otherness of the foe is heightened, not negated. But in fact, the use of violence to destroy the other means that one has in fact become very like that other one hopes to destroy. The only question becomes who destroys whom, even though each calls one's own side good and the other side evil. "Good" violence and "evil" violence are equally destructive in their effects. To be sure, in "just wars" the "good" side uses violence to destroy the ongoing evil of the other side, so that presumably the winning of the war by the "good" side means an end to violence. In historical fact, however, no war seems to have ended violence. Like the hydra-headed dragon, new forms of violence are born through the so-called vanquishing of the violent other. And the violence and its attendant anxiety continue.

Yet another response to the violence experienced through solidarity is not to conform oneself to violence, but to deny one's participation in it. This happens through an extreme individualization of the self, as if one were not relationally constituted. In such cases, violence is "out there," externalized as if it had no effect upon the self at all. Violence is isolated to overt acts committed by "those people," or "inner cities," or "unjust nations." The response of denial entails a passivity to violence that may be the opposite extreme from the response that uses violence to fight violence. But just as the violent response increases the level of violence, so does the passive response. The passive response leaves unexamined one's own participation and benefit from structures of violence, and so implicitly condones the continuation of such structures. The denial of one's own implication through solidarity in the forms of violence in one's society constitutes an additional act of violence. And violence and its attendant anxiety continue unabated.

The most devastating response to violence, of course, is one's own destruction by it. This can take the form of an unrelieved fearfulness of life and society that inhibits the development of one's self-strength. It can be the physical and/or psychical maiming of one's selfhood. Ultimately it can be the loss of one's life as violence rips apart the sustaining bodily structure of life. When violence and its perpetrators are thus successful in their wreaking of ill-being, then the results reverberate throughout the species, raising yet again the levels of violence above the levees built to control it. Anxiety increases.

Dostoyevsky presented an ameliorating response to violence that offered his own answer of hope. He moved beyond solidarity as suffering to solidarity as compassion, as feeling with all others, as discerning love. The transition from one to the other involved the capacity to recognize the web of existence through which we are bound together, to raise it from subliminal to conscious levels. Dostoyevsky's vision was of solidarity become conscious of itself, and living according to this consciousness through compassion.

In an odd twist, such a response involves a conformity to violence, even as does the dysfunctional response that deals with violence by becoming a part of it. But in the Dostoyevskian mode, the conformity does not sacrifice the separate self. Rather, it recognizes the fuller nature of the self as relational, as "self-and-other." Through the self-transcendence of empathy and imagination, the ontological connectedness to the other is lifted to consciousness. Insofar as the one to whom one thus relates is violent or suffering from violence, then the relating self empathically accepts this violence into itself. This is compassion, a "feeling with" that at the same time longs and works for the well-being of the other and therefore the self. Such a dynamic may well underlie the Christian interpretation of Christ on the cross identifying with all sin and sinners, and therefore able to redeem all sinners from sin. Conformity with the sin is an essential step in transformation. In the Dostoyevskyian version, empathic identification with the other allows envisioning the well-being of the other (and therefore the self) through love, and therefore empowers actions toward this well-being. One becomes "one" with the other for the sake of transformation toward an inclusive well-being. The conformity to the other, then, becomes a compassionate will toward well-being.

My own suggestion, to be developed in the final chapter, is that forgiveness is essential as a response to violence if one is to break the cycle of violence and make room for compassion. But before addressing that theme, it is necessary to look at the final aspect of the triadic structure of original sin, which is social inheritance.

SIN

In February, an 11-year-old girl in Westminster was critically injured by a shotgun blast when a male playmate loaded the weapon and fired. And last month, a Garden Grove High School student pleaded guilty to involuntary manslaughter for arming himself with his older brother's handgun and killing a 9-year-old friend.

—*Los Angeles Times*
Monday, March 29, 1993

7

SIN THROUGH
SOCIAL INHERITANCE

S in through violence speaks to the innate bent toward aggression that threads its way through each human individual; sin through solidarity expresses the unity of the race as a whole, and the sense in which each is implicated in the actions of all, whether strongly or slightly. In a sense, the solidarity theme has spatial connotations, referring to the extensiveness of the human race. The third aspect of original sin is more temporally oriented, for it addresses the sense in which the sins of one generation are passed on to the next. Through our social heritage the particular forms of sin that are embodied in a society's institutions to protect the privileges of a dominant group deeply influence the structures of consciousness and conscience of each new generation. Thus institutional forms of cultural life play a strong role in the transmission of sin from generation to generation.

The interconnectedness of all existence not only provides a means for expressing the solidarity of the race, and therefore mutual participation in one another's good or ill, it also gives a peculiar ability to express the dynamics of inherited sin through institutional means. If Dostoyevsky gave expression to the role of solidarity, Walter Rauschenbusch and, once again, Reinhold Niebuhr are eminent guides for the task of illustrating the relation between institutions and sin.

In *A Theology for the Social Gospel*,[1] Rauschenbusch dealt simply and forcefully with the social nature of sin and its transmission in a

---

[1] Walter Rauschenbusch, *A Theology for the Social Gospel* (Nashville: Abingdon, 1978).

way somewhat reminiscent of Schleiermacher, but far more oriented toward the pragmatics of social life than toward the metaphysics underlying the phenomenon of sin. He cited both biological and social phenomena as being involved in the transmission of sin. Biologically, we inherit a physical nature with conflicting instincts, and with a great capacity for ignorance, both of which foster inertia and/or inappropriate behavior which, depending upon the degree of intelligence and will involved, lead to sin. But by far the greater factor in the transmission of sin is our embeddedness within a ready-made social system. We draw our ideas, our moral standards, and our spiritual ideals from the social body into which we are born; these are mediated to us by the public and personal institutions that make up the society. The problem is that the social institutions that so form our values in a capitalist society are driven by a greed that readily exploits the laboring classes, and justifies the exploitation through an idealization of its evil practices. And this idealization of evil becomes the norms from which society fashions its moral consciousness. From childhood, persons do not derive their norms for moral action from a disinterested study of good and evil; rather, we absorb our norms from our social environment.

Rauschenbusch does not consider social groups irredeemably evil; to the contrary, he considers them ordinarily to have been created for acceptable ends, but to be peculiarly susceptible to sinister leadership and the never-ending desire for profits. Hence institutions "fall."[2] But as unique composite personalities that span generations, institutions have the power to fashion moral and political principles that cloak their greed with a sort of reasonableness. The practices that actually rob well-being from the many for the coffers of the few become viewed in society as self-justifying norms that shape the behavior of the society in accordance with those norms. Thus the evil of social groups stems from their insatiable greed, their composite personalities that give them a greater force and often a greater length of life than individuals, and their idealization of evil. One might paraphrase Rauschenbusch by saying that "the problem of sin is that it is profitable."

From a contemporary perspective, it is clear that Rauschenbusch's absorbing passion was to expose the capitalistic sins of American society; he did so under a normative vision of the Kingdom of God that entailed shared rather than shirked labor, and full opportuni-

---

[2] Ibid., p. 72.

ties for self-realization for all. War, militarism, landlordism, predatory industries, and finance are the demons he named that shape social institutions toward fostering their own respectability and perpetuation at the expense of justice. Nor did he leave the church out of this combined "Kingdom of Evil"—to the contrary, long before feminists raised the outcry condemning the church's more than 300 years of intense persecution of women, Rauschenbusch named and decried the church's witch hunting centuries as singularly despicable illustrations of the depths of evil to which the church can fall.[3] Nonetheless, Rauschenbusch held a relatively optimistic view of the capacity of institutions to reform. He thought that the democratization of institutions, including the church, would ameliorate their drift into evil. He was convinced that social sins could be greatly lessened by substituting cooperative institutions for corporate institutions. Changing the one-share, one-vote system to a one-person, one-vote system could be the instrument whereby the norms derived from the Kingdom of God could overturn those norms derived from the Kingdom of Evil.

Rauschenbusch focused almost entirely on an economic understanding of sin, and while he himself did not see the psychic structures of racism and sexism that accompany and undergird the classism of economic systems, he would not have been surprised by their depth and extent. To the contrary, he would undoubtedly judge the social acceptability of both sexism and racism as prime illustrations of the "idealization of evil" through which evil is turned to apparent good for the sake of perpetuating privilege and profit.

Rauschenbusch gave one of the strongest statements in the first half of the twentieth century relating sin to social conditions that form us against the common good, such that each generation corrupts the next.[4] Indeed, with the exception of Reinhold Niebuhr, not until the emergence of the various liberation theologies in the 1960's was theological attention in America focused so strongly on the need for a radical economic restructuring of society.

Perhaps the deepest difference between Rauschenbusch's *A Theology for the Social Gospel* and Niebuhr's *Moral Man and Immoral Soci-*

---

[3] Ibid., p. 84.

[4] He was, however, not alone in his efforts. The "Chicago School" of the early twentieth century, under the leadership of such persons as Shailer Mathews, was also calling for social reform as an inherent part of Christian witness.

ety[5] is in the optimism and pessimism of the respective works. While quite clear-eyed concerning the deep rootedness of power and greed in capitalistic society, Rauschenbusch nonetheless fostered a hope that the opposing moral power of the Kingdom of God as preached by Jesus and recaptured by the church could provide a sufficient opposing moral force to the avarice of capitalistic institutions. By the democratization of such institutions, so that voting power belonged to individual persons rather than to shares, he thought that the power of greed could be broken. Niebuhr held to no such hope. Rather, the very phenomenon of institutions, whether economic or political or national or international, entails the necessity that institutions are always less capable of morality than the individuals comprising those institutions. Like Rauschenbusch, Niebuhr detailed the idealization of evil that institutions create for the sake of preserving economic and political privilege, but unlike Rauschenbusch, he saw no power for transformation in institutions qua institutions. The basic reason is that to Niebuhr institutions, unlike individuals, have but flickering powers of self-transcendence, and without transcendence, no moral action is possible. This compares with the anthropology I outlined in chapter one, for there we saw that Niebuhr considers humankind to be a combination of nature and spirit, with spirit, through the means of mind, being the capacity for transcendence. Insofar as transcendence is not limited to spirit, but pervades the whole being of a person, body and soul, the person is capable of moral action. But since the composite personalities of institutions have no centralized power of mind, neither do they have the capacity for transcendence. And since morality stems from transcendence, without transcendence only the raw collective egoism of the group is left. The crucial ingredient for moral action is simply missing. Thus it is pointless to hope for the creation of truly moral groups; one can only hope to bring individual pressure to bear upon groups to conform themselves to the morality of justice as envisaged by individuals.

Collective groups are little more than collective egoisms, working out the avaricious interests of the dominant powers under various rationales devised by reason. Hypocrisy and coercion are endemic to collective existence, and internal peace is invariably gained at the price of internal justice. Thus in a way that parallels Karl Barth's

---

[5] Reinhold Niebuhr, *Moral Man and Immoral Society: A Study in Ethics and Politics* (New York: Charles Scribner's Sons, 1934).

resounding "no" to humankind's religious pretensions, Reinhold Niebuhr uttered his own "no" to humankind's social pretensions to a moral order.

Far from leading to a passivism, however, Niebuhr advocated realistic planning that took full account of the limitations of all institutions. He argued for the just use of coercion, through nonviolent means when possible, toward the goal of equal justice in society. Given the complexity of the interrelatedness of society, he fully recognized that even nonviolent means would nonetheless entail violent effects. Yet the issue was never a case of violence versus peace, but what forms of violence could be tolerated to overcome a social "peace" that coercively maintained itself through the condoned violence of injustice. His concluding sections of the book, written in the early 1930's, sound like a prophetic description of Martin Luther King, Jr. and the civil rights movement of the 1960's. Indeed, *Moral Man and Immoral Society* is in many respects a precursor to the liberation theologies that would come thirty and forty years later.

Rauschenbusch spoke of groups as a kind of communal human being, a composite personality with a communal mind of its own and endowed with power and endurance much greater than that of the individual person.[6] If the first half of *A Theology for the Social Gospel* gives a sustained account of the greed and perverted spiritual authority of the "kingdom of evil," the latter half speaks hopefully of the church "as the social factor of salvation," even though this is mitigated by the caution that the church as institution often has, does, and undoubtedly still will fall prey to the perversion of power into privilege. But the church is the bearer of the transforming message of the Kingdom of God, and so it can be the instrument of God not only for its own reformation and good, but for the continuous transformation of society as well.

There is nothing in *Moral Man and Immoral Society* to indicate that Niebuhr considers the church any better than other social groups, although he certainly addresses a more positive ecclesiology in the second volume of *The Nature and Destiny of Man* ten years later. But in the earlier work, groups are necessarily immoral when judged by individual standards, since the group "mind" is one where reason is entirely in the service of the group's self-interest. There is little or no redeeming group-transcendence. The correction of society,

---

[6]See p. 71 of *A Theology for the Social Gospel.* Rauschenbusch's indebtedness to Josiah Royce's communal vision is evident in this section.

be it an institution or a nation, needs to come from individuals who understand the limitations of groups, and can bend the groups toward greater social justice. In the nature of the case, those who are marginalized within the group or those who stand totally outside the group are more apt to see through the group hypocrisies than those who directly benefit from the group's exercise of power.

The net effect of Rauschenbusch and Niebuhr is their cogent delineation of the role of society itself in the transmission of sin, albeit each had a quite different assessment of the status and possibilities of groups for good. But in both Rauschenbusch and Niebuhr there is no doubt that sin is mediated to society through the very structures of society. Both oppose the group to the individual, see the group as wielding enormous power over the individual, and recognize the greater temporal longevity that insures that a social group exercises its power over a span of generations. Both demonstrate that individuals are born into a situation where, in Rauschenbusch's words, "hereditary social evils are forced on the individual embedded in the womb of society," whereby the individual will draw "ideas, moral standards, and spiritual ideals from the general life of the social body."[7] When that society inevitably infects its progeny with hypocrisies designed to hide the violence of the privileged, then those who inherit such hypocrisies will themselves believe and indulge them. The societies will be the bearers of sin to which the children will adhere even before they have the means of assent. This is analogous to the traditional doctrine of original sin, where all persons since Adam are corrupted by sin before they have the means to exercise either consent or denial toward the corrupting sin.

Just as relational philosophy provides the ontological grounding that supports Dostoyevsky's insights into the solidarity of humanity, even so relational thinking supports Rauschenbusch and Niebuhr in their analysis of the effect of institutions upon individuals. What relational thinking can add is the dynamics that make social institutions so powerful in their effects, supplementing sociological analyses of institutions with suggestions concerning their ontological structure. This, in turn, will suggest the power of institutions to shape the consciousness and conscience of each individual within her or his sphere of influence. Relational thought underscores just how

---

[7] Ibid., p. 60.

the social structures of the world are implicated in mediating the predisposition to sin.

Niebuhr drew an analogy between the individual and the group, arguing that the individual was composed of nature and spirit, with spirit providing the basis of transcendence and hence of morality, while the composite individual known as the group is to a major degree devoid of spirit, and hence only weakly capable of moral action. Relational thinking likewise makes an analogy between the individual and the group, but arrives at somewhat different conclusions. These will affect the understanding of the group's role in the transmission of sin.

As indicated earlier, the individual person is already a complex organism comprised of many sub-organisms such as a circulatory system, various organs, cells, and molecules. Mind (or soul, or spirit) is marked by its capacity for novelty, and hence its capacity for consciousness and therefore the awareness of transcendence. But this capacity is gained at the price of a certain instability, so that something like mind can exist only when sustained by the stability of the body. Thus the personal sense of subjectivity that comes from consciousness is both fed by the supporting structure of the body, and also irradiates the body with the unity of personality. There are clearly analogies with Niebuhr's anthropology of nature and spirit, but the difference is in the relational structure that connects not only the various aspects of the self, but the self with the wider world. As already shown in chapter two, the transcendence that is here called a centered consciousness emerges horizontally in continuity with the world through relation rather than vertically in a discontinuity with the world.

If the closely interconnected structure of the body is required for the sustenance of mind, and if mind is associated with spirit, then one can understand Niebuhr's contention that groups cannot participate in morality to the same extent as persons. There is no way that a group structure can replicate the deeply interconnected structure of a body, and so sustain the emergence of mind.

But an alternative way of considering the situation in a relational world is to view a group organically rather than in terms of discrete individuals who have come together for some common purpose. We are accustomed to valuing the human person as the highest and most complex form of evolutionary development, but perhaps groups are a yet more complex form. In that case, something other than "mind" may be involved in the organic unity of a group such as an institution or a government. Just as the cells that make up the human body are both deeply connected to the whole identity of the body, and yet discernibly separate, perhaps persons who make up institutions function in ways that are organically essential to the life of the institution, even though only a portion of these functions may be known to the person.

The breakdown in the analogy between the way a human body functions and the way a group functions is that in the human body there is normally but one center of consciousness, whereas in a group there are as many centers of consciousness as there are persons involved in the group. If we consider the group organically, then this difference has enormous implications for the complexity of group life.

The person operates through subjectivity, which is centered in consciousness, but diffused throughout the body. Would it not be the case that a group operates through intersubjectivity, and that this, too, is diffused throughout the group? Perhaps an organism operating through intersubjectivity rather than subjectivity alone simply does not need "a" mind, since in fact it has a multiple mind. What is needed is the organizational structure that conforms its "multiple-mindedness" to the purposes of the group. In small groups, this structure can be very simple, perhaps requiring little more than consensus through conversation. But the larger the group, the more complex the skeletal structure of organization is required. Often liberationist groups have considered hierarchical forms of governance to be a prime tool for reinforcing the power of privilege, but while hierarchies can certainly be used in this way, they are not inherently evil. Rather, they may witness to the complex requirements of structuring very large groups. But whether consensual or hierarchical, whether small or large, all groups operate in and through intersubjectivity, mediated by the organizing structure.

Institutions and social organizations work through the intersubjectivity created by concentric rings of participants, governed by the dynamic force of a rather fluid mission, or purpose for being. Each person associated with the group has some sense of the group's purpose, and how he or she fits into that purpose. No matter how separate the person's private life seems from the institution, the relation to the institution cannot be totally compartmentalized. The person must deal with the relational effects of the institution upon the whole of who the person is. Likewise, the person contributes to what the institution is, whether in a major or minor way.

In a relational world, the uniqueness of the individual becomes a factor in the total identity of the institution. So then, each member of the institution participates not only in personal identity, but in group identity.

This participation means that each individual within the organization reflects the purposes of the organization from a unique perspective. And this reflection not only affects the individual, but the institution as well. The peculiar power of intersubjectivity is the sense in which institutional purpose is reflected myriads of times as if in some great hall of mirrors created by all of its participants. This reflection process need not be explicitly conscious for its effectiveness; it is enough that one has absorbed the institutional purpose to whatever degree into the internal structures of one's identity, and then, in the naturalness of a relational world, woven that purpose into the projections of one's own influence upon others. Within the institution, this reflection-projection process creates the peculiar intersubjectivity of the institution, nuancing and intensifying the institutional purpose, and therefore creating corporate consciousness. This in turn conveys the power of the institution's psychic impact on society as a whole. This psychic impact is woven into the physical or material effects of the institution as it carries out its reason for being.

Agency in institutional existence is diffuse, shared, and delegated. It can take the form of hierarchy similar to that which exists in an individual person, where there is a unique governing center coordinating the relationality of all its parts, and of course the greater the size and complexity of the institution, the more dependent the institution must be on the greater efficiency of hierarchical modes. This creates the complicating factor that an institution may indeed come into existence through recognition of the full individuality of its constituent subjects, but as the institution grows, its very continuation may depend upon adapting to the dynamics of structures with minimal recognition of individual subjectivity. A fully consensual operation that capitalizes upon the full subjectivity of each member of the group presupposes an intimacy within the group that itself depends upon a limitation of size.

Small groups can operate wholly according to communal consciousness,[8] but large groups require some recourse to corporate

---

[8] Witness the base Christian communities of Latin America as detailed in works such as *Ecclesiogenesis* (Maryknoll: Orbis Books, 1981) by Leonardo Boff.

consciousness. And corporate consciousness by definition overrides the subjectivity of its members, even when it presupposes that subjectivity. To carry this analysis back to Rauschenbusch's notion of thoroughly democratizing institutions as a way of countering their propensity toward exploitation of their workers, such democratization can form a check at best, since it cannot eliminate the practical need for hierarchical forms of leadership in large institutions.

The intersubjectivity of an institution allows a peculiar manipulation of that intersubjectivity for individual or specialized group advantage. A diffuse complexity of agency can easily mask personal responsibility; intersubjectivity can be used to hide one's subjectivity. That is, while institutions are more powerful than individuals, exerting greater social force, their looser and intersubjective structures lend themselves to manipulation of that social force by individuals. Thus the immorality of groups so graphically portrayed by Niebuhr does not necessarily depend upon an incapacity of the group for transcendence; to the contrary, it comes about as members of the group use the group to deny their own transcendence and hence use the group as a socially acceptable means of exercising violence.

Thus responsibility itself is created and shared through the intersubjectivity of the institution, but in varying degrees, depending upon the particular institutional structure. Those in places of hierarchical leadership bear a greater responsibility than others. But given the intersubjective nature of the institution, it is not possible to participate in an institution without in some way participating in the responsibility for the institutional effects for good or for ill. All who participate in an institution bear a real responsibility, to one degree or another, for what the institution is.

In any form, institutional agency is created through intersubjectivity; it is a cumbersome agency, because diffuse. At the same time, its compounded complexity of intersubjectivity gives it power that is greater than that of a single individual, even though it may be subverted by an individual. Intersubjectivity differs from a person's subjectivity in and through this different order of complexity. It entails a multiply nuanced and mirrored and repeated intentionality of purpose that exercises its corporate influence on the rest of society, particularly those within its immediate environs.

Institutions themselves, however, are hardly the final word, for they contribute to larger groups that are more loosely organized to create a culturally defined society as a whole, bound together as a unit through mutually albeit somewhat loosely reinforced language and customs. Again, responsibility is diffuse, permeating the inter-subjectivity that actually and dynamically creates the whole, of whatever proportions that whole might be. We live in a Chinese-nesting-box world of interconnected societies, all of which impinge upon the forming consciousness of every individual. Subjectivity, or the unique mode of existence that belongs to individuals, is replaced by intersubjectivity at the level of institutions and society.

The way intersubjectivity works both personally and institutionally can be illustrated by the peculiar dynamics that occur when one begins a new association with an institution. When this happens, a person encounters a whole new configuration of her or his personal past. Personal history is contextualized in a different way, being intertwined with the histories of all others in the institution, and by the history of the institution as a whole. Whereas previously these relations were peripheral to the formation of one's identity, the new association gives them a heightened prominence in the continuing formation of identity. Part of the jarring sense of transition is the ontological demand at subliminal levels to respond to newly relevant relationships, weaving them into one's own continuing becoming self. New associations place new demands and invitations upon one's becoming. Personal participation in the intersubjectivity of an institution is the recontextualization of one's personal identity. But by the same token, one's own energies become newly interwoven with the institution and those associated with it, adding a new dimension to its character which will be manifest at greater or lesser intensities, depending upon the size of the institution. The complexity in the resulting intersubjectivity is increased still further by the overarching reality of the institution, which is woven not simply through the intersubjectivity of its members, but through the tendrils of its relationship to all of its constituencies in its own unique trajectory of time.

The psychic power of the forms of intersubjectivity that create institutions and societies lies in their being channels for a multiply reinforced group structure of consciousness that forms a common grid for interpreting experience in the world. Intersubjectivity itself creates the normative structures whereby individual subjects order their lives. Further, these structures are not externally imposed, they are internally inherited through the relationality of existence, contributing to the formation of every subjectivity that receives them. To be born into a particular society is to inherit ways of forming values, of interpreting the world, and of acting in the world. Thus the gift of intersubjectivity to its children is to provide the parameters within which consciousness becomes self-consciousness, ordered into a world.

The account of sin prefacing this chapter deals with the sins of children who engaged in murderous violence. One assumes that these children were raised in an American culture that exalts violence, particularly as an answer to violence. Child-oriented cartoons are often based upon a story line of violence humorously portrayed as tormentors are tormented in return. Childhood computer games rack up scores based upon the number of "killings" that have been skillfully accomplished. Films oriented toward young persons present violence as an answer to the problems of life, and toys meant for small boys are detailed replicas of instruments of war. Throughout these and other modes, violence is shown to be the norm for dealing with the problems of life. The line between fantasy and reality for children is not always so clearly drawn. In addition, there is the caution from Irenaeus Eibl-Eibesfeldt given in chapter five concerning the ability of violent fantasy to arouse one's instinctive aggressions beyond the ability of fantasy alone to resolve. Given the presence of weapons of violence, norms that sanction their use, and the presenting occasion of perceived violation of their own well-being, the children in the news report murdered or attempted to murder. The culture creates the conditions within which children become murderers.

Based upon the analysis in chapter five, the social endorsement of violence is not written on a clean slate. If a bent toward violence is built into the species, then the issue is how we use that violence. It surely has the potential to create conditions of ill-being for self and others, but this is not necessary, given the human capacity for bonding with others through empathy and imagination. Empathy and imagination together can influence the channeling of aggressiveness into nonviolent modes, whether as an energy, or passion, or, as Kathleen Greider suggests, into a synergy with love.[9] But it is also more than possible for that bent toward violence to be fostered in its own right, until it becomes a normative and desirable response to problematic situations in the world.

---

[9] Kathleen Greider, "'Too Militant?': Aggression, Gender, and the Construction of Justice," *Occasional Paper* No. 10, Vol. 3, No.2, (April 1993), published by the School of Theology at Claremont.

Each of the agencies involved in molding the norm of violence that leads children to become murderers bears some of the responsibility involved in the fate of those youngsters. To apply the theory of intersubjectivity here developed, that influence was exercised not only in the products that directly reached the children, but also through the acceptability of violence that threaded its way through each institution. For example, those who create, market, and present films for children that exalt violence develop a double intersubjectivity: that which is created in the various companies involved, and that which emanates from all of the employees of the company into the wider society, creating the culture. The originating writers, responding to directives received from their employers, spend their creative energies imagining infinite variations on the theme of injury and retribution: violence. Their internalization of the acceptability of fantasized violence is intensified by its acceptability to their fellow employees, and perhaps justified by the catharsis for violence that fantasy can provide. Distinctions may be made between children and adults concerning the amount of stimuli that can be cathartically handled, but even when this happens, no account is given to the sense in which the product joins a multitude of other influences, all giving the message of violence toward others as an acceptable response to anger. Rather, the production of the violent film is acceptable for the sake of profit and livelihood. Thus within the company itself, violence as norm in the mode of entertainment for children becomes self-evidently justified.

But attitudes formed in the workplace are not necessarily left in the office or shop. Even when the controlled violence of entertainment is seen as a cathartic way of dealing with the increasing violence of society, the attitude of sanctioning fantasy violence can in fact be involved in increasing actual violence in our streets and schools. The close intersubjectivity of the working group disperses to become part of the intersubjectivity of personal groups, and of the society as a whole.

Meanwhile, of course, programs of fictional violence (and photographed violence in news programs) are shown on numerous television stations, beamed into the homes of millions of children. Here the norm of violence as acceptable entertainment contributes to shaping the developing subjectivity of the watching children, forming structures of interpreting the world, and forming the structures of conscience. Hopefully for most children this violence is countered by other values, so that it is subordinated within the complexity of their developing personalities. But for some children—perhaps the children in our illustration—it remains as an unchecked norm, ready to govern behavior when frustrations occur and a gun is available. They live out in reality the norms which the inventors thought belonged only to fantasy, entertainment, and profit.

The very culture into which one is born is made up of various modes of intersubjectivity that are themselves woven into the wider intersubjectivity of the culture itself. Since intersubjectivity is the mirroring of group purpose back and forth from person to person, multiplied a thousandfold, there is an enormous force for repetition of those values. Infants are born with the ability to structure the world, but how they do so as they develop is through the ready-made systems of interpretation that they breathe into their growing selves. Intersubjectivity provides the structures of individual consciousness, and the value systems that allow one to organize one's responsiveness to the world.

When, then, the institutions of society are organized around a purpose of maintaining privilege or profit in the sense so well described by Rauschenbusch and Niebuhr, and when this purpose is rationalized through an idealization that renders the purpose normative, then these values affect not only those immediately participating in the institution, but in the society as a whole within which the institution is embedded. Just as persons tend to have a double focus in their actions, which includes both their own and their contextual good, even so do institutions. Intersubjectivity magnifies the force of the institutional idealization of its purpose, and projects that idealization into the wider society as an operative norm. Individuals raised within such a society internalize the norms, thus supporting them and ensuring their continued perpetuation.

Since it is the individual *self*-consciousness that is so formed, it becomes constitutive of the self, and difficult to transcend. One's actions from this center of consciousness will then actualize the norms, perpetuating them relative to one's own position and perspective within the grid of the intersubjective society at large. By definition, the inherited norms cannot be questioned prior to their enactment: one is caught in sin without virtue of consent. Original sin simply creates sinners.

The individual inheritance that includes a disposition toward violence built into human nature, the solidarity of the race whereby we participate in one another's sin, and the social structures that mediate values contributing to ill-being, combine to create a situation for every new generation analogous to that suggested by the doctrine of original sin. We are indeed in a sorry plight, and our final two chapters will explore the consequences of this plight in the phenomenon of guilt, and the possibilities for resolution through forgiveness and transformation.

SIN

A sailor who killed a gay shipmate suffered child abuse in a broken home and hated homosexuals. He inflicted injuries as severe as if his victim had been killed in "a high-speed auto accident or low speed airplane crash," then told an investigator he'd do it again, a court-martial was told here Tuesday.

—*Los Angeles Times*
Wednesday, May 26, 1993

PART 3
RESPONSE TO SIN

CHAPTER
8

GUILT AND FREEDOM

A bent toward violence built into the human species, the solidarity of the race wherein each is affected by the deeds of all others and affects the future of all others, and finally the unique structures of intersubjectivity that mediate the values of one generation to the next, all conspire to create conditions for each human individual that are analogous to the ancient concept of original sin. To be human is to be embroiled in sin before one even has the means to assent. And the embroilment, in a relational world, means that one has internalized attitudes that lead to actions of ill-being. One is constituted throughout one's relational being as sinner.

But if one is so constituted even before one can meaningfully consent to these values or actions, why is the situation sin rather than simply being the tragic structure of evil? Why not speak of original evil instead of original sin? What can guilt mean where there is sin without consent?

Guilt is involved when the freedom to transcend the structures of ill-being is present, and one does not transcend those structures. This means, somewhat paradoxically, that one can be a sinner "innocently," without guilt, and this applies to infants, small children, and those whose physiological conditions do not allow normal maturation. But normally there comes a point where transcendence of one's participation in evil is possible, and at that point, guilt is incurred.

The critical importance of retaining the terminology of sin is that sin, unlike evil, entails human responsibility and human hope. Simply to call a situation evil can lead to passivity or paralysis with regard to that evil. Evil overwhelms us, often as an impersonal force of fate. But sin is a human category, created in, through, and by us—and therefore sin is potentially a reality that, no matter how intricate, can yield to transformation. To name something as sin is to say, "this ought not to be the case." Such a judgment witnesses to a better alternative, and offers the catalytic hope of transformation, even though our original involvement in sin takes place before we are capable of transcending it.

The above, of course, is a pragmatic reason for naming moral evil as sin. But just as I developed a relational ontology in order to account for the pervasive condition of moral evil, even so I must show how that ontology supports the attribution of guilt, and so merits the terminology of sin as well as evil. To do so requires exploration of the category of freedom, since guilt is a corollary of freedom.

A contemporary challenge to an ontology of freedom is that despite the pervasive human experience of at least the freedom of choosing between options, there are both scientific and philosophical arguments claiming that what we call freedom is in reality simply our ignorance or uncertainty concerning all of the causes that affect us. But if there is no freedom, then neither is there sin. There is only the evil of what must necessarily be the case. If there is no sin, then neither is there responsibility, and guilt is a misplaced phenomenon requiring only the services of a good psychologist or philosopher to rid one of its discomfort. And if there is neither responsibility nor guilt, then there is no hope for transformation of the conditions we name as evil so long as evil does not noticeably affect our comfort level. It is essential, then, for the theology of sin to be based on an ontology of freedom.

Freedom, however, has been variously defined. One powerful definition is the freedom to develop according to one's highest potential. To be a human being is to be gifted with certain characteristics and abilities, and freedom is understood as the possibility of bringing these characteristics and abilities to expression within the context of a community. This definition of freedom is particularly operative in theologies of liberation. It is, however, a sociological definition of freedom that itself depends upon a more basic definition rooted in ontology. The sociological understanding of freedom depends upon an ability to develop one's potential within a context where this development may be hindered or facilitated by self or others. This implies that the unfolding of one's potential is not an automatic happenstance of nature; it is instead a given possibility within one's nature. Whether or not it happens depends upon the ontological freedom of self and others to choose among options. Thus a definition of freedom as the ability to realize one's potential rests upon a more fundamental definition of freedom as the ability to choose. It is this freedom that must be established within the same ontology of relationships that supports a new reading of original sin.

To develop an ontology of freedom, I turn first to an illustration of the experience of freedom when all appearances suggest only raw determinism. The illustration comes from the profound account of freedom told by Viktor Frankl, survivor of Auschwitz, in *Man's Search for Meaning.*[1] Herded toward Auschwitz in a cattle car, he arrived at that place of wretchedness only to encounter a divestiture of all he held dear. His wife was torn from him, sent to the showers. "There is your wife," said a fellow prisoner that evening, pointing to the black smoke rising. Frankl's manuscript, sewn into the lining of his coat, was found and ripped to shreds: his life's work, gone in moments. His warm clothing was taken, every hair on his body was shaved off, and he began harshly regimented days and months and years of forced labor, clad in rags, and living on thin soup. Viktor Frankl, of all persons, might speak of determinism in a life totally robbed of freedom.

But a most memorable passage in the book concerns the forced march of his work party, made up of skeletal survivors of enslavement, on a late winter afternoon. It was then that he saw it: the violet sky of winter against the white snow. Connecting sky and snow on the horizon was a single bare tree, lacy in its blackness against that white snow, that violet sky. Its shape was exquisitely graceful, tracing the connectedness of twig, branch, trunk, and establishing the connectedness of earth and sky. He was stunned by its beauty. When every element of his humanity had been brutally stripped from him, and every moment of his life had been bitterly planned, he still had the ability to respond to beauty. And he knew himself free.

One might question whether or not what he experienced as his free response to the tree was itself determined by his earlier life experiences. Surely, his response was conditioned by his personal

---

[1] Viktor E. Frankl, *Man's Search for Meaning* (New York: Harper and Row, 1974).

and ethnic past rich in Judaism. But an ontology of relationships must argue that while freedom is necessarily conditioned by one's past and one's context, freedom cannot be reduced to those causes.

The ontology of relationships maintains that the very possibility of relationships depends upon the ability to respond to relationships, and that this "response-ability" is at the core of every moment of our lives. This response-ability qualifies everything that exists at its most fundamental level in a relational world. Even a rock is composed of electrons and atoms and molecules that in themselves have a response-ability relative to their past and to their environs. The rock changes, yielding to erosion and radioactive decay. The aggregate of the rock does not have freedom in a human sense, but in its very constitution, it has a response-ability that represents a miniscule indeterminism on a chain that includes, at its other end, what we call human freedom. This freedom is an ability to question the givenness of oneself and one's world; it is self-transcendence exercised through one's response-ability.

Indeterminism is a blind responsiveness to influences; freedom is the ability to lift this responsiveness to consciousness. It was precisely this response-ability and responsiveness in the complexity of his humanity that Viktor Frankl exercised when he exulted in gratitude at the beauty of the tree. And that form of freedom is extinguishable only by death. To be human is to experience freedom at the core of one's being.

But that freedom is indeed conditioned. Frankl's freedom was vastly restricted, and while most of us do not experience the coercion that so diminished his freedom, we too deal with a freedom that is shaped by context. If this were not so, relationality would be meaningless. One does not have a set amount of pure freedom, as if freedom were a substance that could be poured into a measuring cup and doled out when needed. Rather, the influx of relation that goes into our moment-by-moment creation forces a response that is yet paradoxically free.

It is a forced response, because apart from a response to relation, there is no coordination of relation, and hence no coming-to-be of the relational reality. Responding to relation is the creation of the self. But it is a free response, because within the context of precisely these relations, *how* one responds rests with the self-determination of the responding entity. There are parameters, to be sure: Freedom is always conditioned, and there is no possibility of an unconditioned freedom within this ontology. The parameters of freedom may be wide or exceedingly narrow. But the parameters, by definition, are multiple, and therefore force decision making among alternatives.

The multiplicity of the parameters follows from the multiplicity of relationships. In a previous chapter, I developed an ontology that describes our world—our universe—as a place created in and through the fact of everything affecting everything else. In the nineteenth century, Feuerbach said that we are what we eat; in the twentieth century, we might add that we are as we relate. Since a vast multitude of influences from throughout the universe bombards each of us at every moment, the possibilities for integrating these relationships are necessarily multiple. Given this vast multiplicity of relationships converging on every becoming moment, there is an inevitable variable attendant upon how the becoming moment responds. In low-grade organisms this variability is no more than some degree of indeterminism. In highly complex individuals, such as human persons, that variability can be called freedom.

Freedom relates always to the present rather than to the past or the future. It is as if freedom is like the moving edge of the crest of a wave. While a wave is cresting, that crest is neither in the calm shallows between the cresting wave and the shore, nor is it in the depths of the ocean behind: It is purely a present phenomenon relative to the wave. Once it is completed, it no longer exists. The situation is similar with freedom; it can only be experienced in the present.

Freedom is not a quality particularly pertaining to the future, for that future has only possible, not actual, existence. Possibilities themselves exercise no freedom; they simply are what they are. Likewise, an examination of the past will not reveal freedom, for the past is the record of what was done with freedom as it itself became a determining influence for its successors.

Given the fact that freedom, or self-determinacy, is always a present fact in the process of succeeding itself, then it is no wonder that persons who look to the past to discover whether or not freedom exists find that their search reveals only determinism. What must be recognized is that determinism is itself a complex reality consisting of three temporal forms.

Determinism relative to the past is the cumulative stubborn facticity (to use Whitehead's memorable phrase) of what was done when that past was itself present. As past, it exercises a determinative effect on what may become.

Determinism relative to the future refers to the influence of vision. Present perceptions of what *can* be done have an influence on what *will* be done. This determinism is, of course, far looser than that laid down by the past, but like the past, it has a role to play in determining the parameters within which the present may develop.

The form of determinism belonging to the present is self-determinism, which is, of course, freedom. Insofar as the parameters laid down by past and future are multiply complex, it rests with the becoming present to resolve the variables into one specific actuality. In the process of becoming, the present event must exercise some degree of self-determining power. But once it has become, the event is determinate, determining now in its own turn the parameters for the next moment of freedom.

Given this freedom, there is an established basis for responsibility for one's actions. If there is responsibility, then there is also guilt to the degree that one's use of freedom contributes to the ill-being of oneself or any other. Guilt itself is a complex concept relating not only to freedom, but to control, to transgressions of boundaries, and to what I will call an ontological condition that emerges with the maturation of freedom. It should be strongly noted that feeling guilty is not necessarily connected with ontological guilt, since one can easily feel guilty from a variety of causes other than sin.

Historically, Christianity associated guilt with the ability or failure to exercise control. If a situation is amenable to one's control, one is answerable for the exercise of that control. Augustine's famous dictum, "all evil is the result of sin and its punishment," reflects this connection of guilt and control. Insofar as all humans could be identified with Adam and Eve in the moral evil that distorted human nature, then all humans were held responsible for the consequent natural and physical disasters. This was an original guilt that went hand in hand with original sin, and that affected all humankind. Hence, as was noted in chapter one, even infants, who have not yet sinned personally, were considered heir to the consequences of this guilt and thus subject to illness and death.

When the doctrine of original sin was lost, the three categories of evil—natural, physical, and moral—remained, but guilt was dissociated from the first two, and mitigated in the third. Guilt was related to control, and since one could do little until our own century about disasters, illness, pain, and death, one simply suffered these things; one was not guilty of them. With regard to moral evil, there was almost a total reversal of the tradition. The tradition said that moral evil caused natural and physical evil; the Enlightenment thinkers said natural and physical evil cause moral evil. Guilt and responsibility for moral evil were correspondingly lessened. One's moral misdeeds were but the natural effect of one's environment, or conditioning; what else could one do? Elements of this thinking survive into the twentieth century, as witnessed by Karl Meninger's famous challenge, "Whatever Became of Sin?"

The trajectory of blameless moral evil, however, has paradoxically been paralleled by another. Insofar as human control over natural and physical phenomena has increased in the twentieth century, the notion of guilt has begun to creep back into issues of natural and physical evil. Literature abounds indicating that we are culpable when it comes to our own illnesses, and that by correct imaging, or eating, or mind-body control, one can and should reverse illness. Perhaps there is some truth to this position, but human mortality also has much to do with the reality of illness and death. Does it not seem like a strange secular return to the Augustinian dictum that all evil is the result of sin and its punishment when illness is made the "fault" of the sufferer?

Insofar as we have increased our control over the environment, we have also extended guilt toward those who suffer from environmental disasters. One is not responsible for earthquakes, tornadoes, or floods—but one *is* responsible for checking out the environmental forces in one's vicinity, and choosing one's housing accordingly. However, to the degree that natural phenomena are somewhat predictable but not controllable, we mitigate the guilt we assign to those who suffer in nature's wake.

Guilt, then, is associated with control, which is itself associated with the freedom of alternative choices. But sin and guilt are not necessarily co-terminous; one is implicated in sin prior to being implicated in guilt. While sin is participation in the ill-being of others, guilt involves the possibility of control over that participation. Infants, for example, are involved in the human solidarity that involves ill-being and well-being, and thus they participate in sin. The child may be a part of society that benefits greatly from exploitation of others—or the child may be victim of gross corporate greed, as happened in the milk scandals brought to public attention in the 1970's. Infants are born into a ready-made situation of the infinite variations of needless violence, and hence by this relational association they are participants in sin. But contrary to the tradition, they participate innocently; they are not yet guilty. Guilt evolves from the growth into greater freedom at a later stage in human development. Insofar as maturation inescapably involves growth of the ability to question oneself and one's actions, then one grows into responsibility, guilt, and the attendant possibilities for transformation.

This growth deals with the third element of original sin that I have proposed, inherited structures of consciousness and conscience. The infant grows, and develops, and her or his personality soon begins to take shape. Much of the development is genetically inherited, but it is clear that environment has a highly significant effect. Infants and small children who are deprived of loving arms to hold them will be blighted in their spiritual development, no matter how excellent their DNA. Environment, including the language that is used to interpret and describe that environment, shapes the structures through which lives are organized and ordered, and this begins in infancy. Children acquire social structures that shape the way they think through the verbal and nonverbal communication patterns that they learn to employ.

Necessarily involved in this structure is a given value system. One effect of original sin is the structuring of one's value system and world in a way that assumes as normative the ill-being of others. The child is not responsible for the way that value system is set up, but the child is response-able to that value system. The child internalizes the system as part of the development of an operative structure of the world. But as the child grows, the capacity for freedom likewise grows.

Initially, as in the child's first "why?", the question is hardly more than a recognition that the influential structures are there. Already this is the beginning of self-transcendence, for recognizing structures is seeing them as being in some respect differentiated from the self. The marvel of this occurrence is that the structures that are differentiated from the self yet form the self; for this reason, a questioning of the structures is already self-transcendence.

This recognition of structure-as-structure grows to the point of evaluation. Emotive responses are interwoven throughout the continuum from recognition to evaluation, with these responses beginning as curiosity and progressing to judgment. There comes a time when the child is capable of questioning the structures that are inherited. This ability marks the dawn of the freedom of transcendence over the structures. This self-transcendence is essential to human freedom, since it allows some degree of control over the effects of those structures upon one. It is at the same time a movement into guilt, since guilt is involved when the freedom to transcend these structures is present, and one does not transcend those structures. I illustrate the point through my own experience.

I was born in New England, and grew up in a town just northeast of Boston. There were very few African Americans in my town, but those few all lived in the same neighborhood. I knew nothing of the bitterness of racism that forced persons of African American ethnicity into preestablished constrictions of their freedom. Was I innocent or guilty in that racism? I answer the question by continuing the story: I went to the movies as a child, and in those days trains were the mode of travel. I loved the glamor of that strange and wondrous milieu, where people boarded trains and crossed the whole continent. White people and black people both got on those trains, but the white people had the tickets, and the black people took them. White people and black people both went to the pullman sleepers, but the white people got into the berths, and the black people held the curtains to make it more comfortable for them to do so. The white people and the black people both used the dining cars, but the white people were seated at the tables, and the black people served them.

I saw these films, and absorbed their racism into the structures of my consciousness, never questioning why the African Americans lived separately in poorer homes, or why their occupations were so predictable in film to film, and in real life as well. But I could question other things; why did I never question this? To the degree that I never questioned, I became a racist at the core of my being, accepting and integrating racist structures of consciousness into my way of being in the world.

Not only did I become a racist, I perpetuated racism by my unthinking support of those structures. And lest this be considered an innocuous form of racism, I suggest that such ingrained attitudes of passive acceptance of a great social evil create the substructure that supports the horrors of torture and lynching when and where they occur. It is analogous to the one hundred stories of a building supporting the existence of the one hundred and first story. It is sin, and entails guilt. It is original sin, in that it is a pre-given structure of ill-being through which we view the world, inherited as the very stuff that forms the world *as* world. It becomes personal sin when, having the ability to question the structure, we fail to do so, and thus support and perpetuate the structure. The freedom to question introduces the reality of guilt.

Before developing this ontology of guilt further, it is necessary to distinguish between ontological guilt and the phenomenon of feeling guilty. Ontological guilt relates specifically to one's personal participation in perpetuating the conditions of original sin. This form of participation in original sin emerges with the maturation of freedom. It entails the ability to transcend the structures of one's world. Guilt follows when one *can* transcend one's own structures of value, but chooses instead to remain immersed within those values. This guilt may be experienced as a feeling of guilt, but since feelings of guilt most often have to do with transgressed boundaries, more often than not ontological guilt does not involve guilt feelings. I will illustrate this subsequently, but since guilt and feeling guilty are so often equated, I must briefly discuss feelings of guilt, which I am tentatively relating to the experience of transgressing boundaries.

Feeling guilty often follows from the sense of having transgressed previously held boundaries, regardless of whether those boundaries were or were not appropriate, and regardless of whether or not one crossed those boundaries willingly. In such cases, the feeling of guilt is very real, but the actuality of guilt may or may not apply. The most egregious examples of feelings of false guilt occur when victims of incest or other forms of abuse assume responsibility for the crime. In these cases, part of the horror of the sin against the victim is that the violence does not end with the actual act, but continues in the internalized violence of feelings of guilt. The feelings are real enough, but they relate not to the culpability of the victim, but to the nature of the crime itself insofar as it violates the victim's own boundaries of selfhood. Feelings of guilt easily accompany transgression of boundaries that define one's sense of acceptable being and behavior. The abuse forces the victim outside such boundaries, so that the feelings of guilt are extensions of the abuse. Thus the abuse is not contained within the moments of the actual infliction of physical and psychological injury—quite to the contrary. Since the abuse invades the inner boundaries of the self, the abuse sets off a cascading system of negative self-esteem transmitted through the medium of guilty feelings.

Less tragic examples of the feelings of guilt accompanying transgression of boundaries are found in the infraction of personal or social mores. To set a diet for oneself is to set boundaries on what one may eat; transgressing the boundaries may result in feelings of guilt. A social group may impose strict standards of dress or behavior as part of its criteria for identity. A member of the group who deviates from these conventions can encounter the uneasiness of disapproval, not simply from the group, but from the internalization of the group standards. The boundaries of identity have been crossed, and the experience of self-disapproval translates into guilty feelings. The guilty feelings are less an indication of sin than an indication of the successful internalization of cultural standards.

Yet another form of feeling guilty that is not related to ontological guilt is found in the experience of grief. A spouse dies; often the remaining spouse will be plagued not only with the awful loss, but with self-recrimination concerning fancied actions that might have prevented the loss. Transgression of boundaries is again involved, but this time in the sense that death has forced the surviving person into a radical reconfiguration of identity, and therefore boundaries. Previously, self-identity included the ongoing relation with the loved one, but that aspect of identity has undergone drastic change. Like the victim of abuse, the survivor has been catapulted against her or his will into a different identity configuration; in both cases, since it is one's *own* identity that is now in question despite one's will, boundaries have been crossed, and one feels guilty.

Ontological guilt is related less to the transgression of boundaries and more to the failure to transcend the boundaries established by original sin. Original sin is the condition whereby, regardless of consent, we participate in and/or contribute to ill-being.

In my previous chapter, I spoke to the situation of children who murder other children in the context of a society that promotes the acceptability of violence as a response to provocations in the world. There I developed the social inheritance through intersubjectivity that contributed to the norms of violence that governed the children. Here I push the issue further to explore the question of guilt. Who is guilty?

Most immediately, insofar as these children were capable of self-transcendence through empathy or imagination, then the children are to that degree responsible for their actions, and guilty. But is their guilt not shared by many others? Someone made guns available to children, and so participates in responsibility. Corporate greed for ever-greater profits from gun sales results in an incredible proliferation of guns throughout American culture, all under the reasoning that if everyone has guns, everyone can protect the self from everyone else, and so honor the sacred "right to bear arms" guaranteed to every American. Do not those who profit from this greed share in the responsibility of murder committed by children?

Violence is embedded deeply within the human psyche, and fantasy concerning violence allows a "safe" projection of the violence into "entertainment." But the well of violence is inexhaustibly deep, forming a basis for insatiable appetites for more and stronger violent fantasies. Do not those who traffic in developing the taste for violence share in the guilt for these children's sin?

And what of the passive population, along with its appointed guardians of the culture? Is not the unbridled worship of violence in the culture aided and abetted by the passive response of most of us to the escalation of violence not only in "entertainment," but on our streets and in our schools?

In short, the children who murdered sinned, and incurred guilt, to the degree that it was possible for them to transcend their impulse to this violence, but did not. The greater guilt, however, rests with those increasingly larger circles that made this action by children not only thinkable, but possible. The American society as a whole shares in the guilt of these murders, and in the malformation of the consciences of children who were capable of turning violent fantasy into violent reality.

The news report beginning this chapter provides a slightly different insight to the issue of violence and guilt. One speculates that two issues were conflated in the sailor's world: homophobia, and child abuse. If the sailor himself was a victim of homosexual child abuse, then the rampant homophobia in the culture would have allowed him to universalize his own particular situation. Powerless over his abuser, he transferred his hatred from his abuser toward all homosexuals. An analogous situation happens for young girls in heterosexual abuse, whose numbers vastly exceed the number of boys who suffer homosexual abuse. Having suffered so violently from one man, distrust is projected upon all men. Even so, one speculates that the abused child who grows into the sailor transferred his hatred of his abuser to the whole category of homosexual men.

Unlike the situation for women, who continue to experience the dominant power of men in society, the sailor grew into a world where his abuser came from a despised minority little protected by law. Violence against homosexuals was tacitly acceptable, whether through "gay-bashing" on the streets or through various forms of discrimination in housing or in the workplace. Such social attitudes encouraged his hatred, which combined with his violence eventually resulted in his murderous rage against an innocent man. Who is guilty?

The sailor, unlike the children in the previous illustration, is an adult, and has the capacity to transcend his situation and his impulses. He did not, and he is guilty. But again, the guilt does not stop with the sailor, it continues into his past where it emanates from his abuser, and into the culture that allows ill-being towards those who are born with a sexual orientation toward persons of their own gender. Guilt is both focused in the murderer and diffused throughout the society. We hold the sailor to moral and legal responsibility for his crime, as well we ought: but when do we hold the homophobic society responsible? When do we hold the abusers of children responsible? Guilt pervades the society as a whole.

The catch-22 of sin and guilt is that by the time one reaches the point of being able to say "this ought not to be the case," one's whole way of experiencing the world has been developed in and through that now negatively judged structure. This is why the ability to judge the structure is a self-transcendence, and not simply a transcendence of the society in which one lives. To the extent that the structures mediate ill-being, one's very selfhood has been formed in sin; at the point where one is capable of transcending and judging the self, one is involved in guilt as well. Original sin becomes personal sin; with the advent of personal sin, there is also the advent of culpability: guilt.

If ontological guilt relates to a refusal to transcend the value structures that form the boundaries of one's existence, and feelings of guilt most often relate to transgressed boundaries, then the paradox obtains that one can avoid feelings of guilt by remaining within the condition of ontological guilt. For example, to live in most portions in the world is to participate in some form of racism relative to ethnic groups on the margins of the power structure and value system of the culture. All who have attained the capacity to transcend the norms and structures of society participate in this racism, most passively, but many actively: all share in the guilt. But to change one's attitudes and actions concerning the racism is to violate the communal norms; it is to transgress boundaries. To begin to change one's attitudes and actions is to risk feelings of guilt relative to what has been and relative to what the society expects. But these feelings of guilt may or may not relate to the actual guilt that one has incurred, which is the fundamental fact of racist oppression.

Thus one might paradoxically avoid feelings of guilt by remaining guilty.

Recognition of one's guilt, whether it be the ontological guilt incurred through solidarity with the human race, or passive guilt through failure to transcend boundaries that work ill-being, or active guilt through personal participation in acts of psychic or physical violence, can surely engender appropriate feelings of guilt. These are to be distinguished from those guilty feelings aroused through transgressions of boundaries that do not work ill-being. The positive aspect of appropriate feelings of guilt is that they function much as pain does in signaling a dysfunction in the body. Feelings of guilt can be the catalyst toward transformation. As such, appropriate guilty feelings are not a stopping place relative to sin, but a transitional space.

Guilt does not reduce violence: To the contrary, the experience of guilt can exacerbate violence. Guilt is a necessary transitional step toward owning complicity in violence, which is at the same time the power to name oneself, and so to gain some measure of control. However, the process of movement from naming complicity and guilt to discovering the positive power of transcendence is not automatic. It is possible to become stuck in guilt as if it were a stopping place rather than a transitional space. Guilt that is not a movement becomes the other side of violence. It is the internalization of the fruits of violence, which itself can build up a pressure that explodes in further external violence. Thus the experience of guilt alone cannot be the answer to the threefold problem of sin derived from the bent toward violence, the solidarity of the race, and structural norms of ill-being. Rather, guilt must give way to forgiveness.

SIN

Each day, thousands of Latinos go to work in Los Angeles-area factories where they ingest toxic dust, expose their unprotected skin to dangerous chemicals and breathe noxious fumes that can destroy lungs and brain cells.

Some knowingly risk their health, so desperate are they to feed their families. Many others toil in ignorance, not fully realizing that they are being exposed to materials that can kill or cripple them.

"There are easily thousands of workers in this county who are exposed to hundreds of thousands of times the allowable level of toxics, and the oversight is a fraction of what it should be," said Dr. Paul J. Papanek, chief of Los Angeles County's toxics epidemiology program. "There is no monitoring to speak of."

—Los Angeles Times
Monday, September 6, 1993

9

FORGIVENESS
AND TRANSFORMATION

Forgiveness may be the most difficult of virtues. To sin against the other is to violate the other; to be sinned against is to be violated. Violation itself has forms as infinite and ugly as the pains it creates, as is manifest in the diversity of news accounts used throughout this investigation. Violation ranges from the intensely personal experience of psychic and/or physical violence against the self or one's loved ones to the most diffuse sense of violation through the pervasiveness of violence in one's culture or world. Violence sets up a chain effect of reactionary response, as is witnessed in the endless retaliatory wars of gangs, tribes, clans, or nations. Forgiveness is an alternative response to violence that has the power to break this cycle.

But what is forgiveness over against violence? I suggest that forgiveness is willing the well-being of victim(s) and violator(s) in the context of the fullest possible knowledge of the nature of the violation. As such, forgiveness holds the possibility of breaking the chain of violence.

In order to develop this suggestion I must first clarify this definition of forgiveness by contrasting it with popular misconceptions of the term, and by developing the significance of each of its three constitutive dimensions: the action of willing well-being, the relation of victim and violator, and the courage of knowledge and remembrance. In the process, the ground of forgiveness in the forms of transcendence developed in chapter two must be made clear: without memory, empathy, and imagination there can be no forgiveness. Second, since violence is the corruption of time, I must show in what sense forgiveness offers a redemption of time, and hence the possibility of transformation. Finally, since sin is both personal and social, forgiveness must be explored in relation to both of these levels of violence.

There are two typical misconceptions regarding forgiveness. The first assumes that to forgive entails feelings of love; the second assumes that to forgive another is to accept the other. Neither of these is substantiated by an investigation of forgiveness that takes full account of the horror of violence. Note that if forgiveness is an action of will toward the well-being of victim and violator in the fullest possible knowledge of the nature of the violation, then forgiveness is fundamentally a matter of intellect rather than of emotions. This means that while forgiveness may very well include the emotional warmth of love, it does not necessarily do so. And indeed, given the enormity of much sin, if feelings of love were required for forgiveness to take place, then where forgiveness is needed most, it would be in shortest supply. How is one to develop authentic feelings of emotional warmth toward one's rapist, or the murderer of one's child, or the political torturers not only of adults, but of children? What kinds of warm feelings can be evoked toward political tyrants who bear the responsibility of catastrophic violence toward vast numbers of people? What sense does it make to feel love toward negligent owners of factories or slums?

If forgiveness depended upon warmth of feeling, we might well be locked forever into experiencing an unending cycle of violence and revulsion. But forgiveness is less a matter of the emotions than a matter of the will. Since violence wounds perpetrators as well as victims, to choose to will the well-being of violators involves willing their own transformation toward the good. And the capacity for transcendence through memory, empathy, and imagination means that one *can* deliberately will well-being, even over against feelings of revulsion and antipathy. Therefore, the release that is possible through the act of willing forgiveness is available even for those who suffer most deeply from sins committed against them. Forgiveness interpreted as feelings of love has little to do with the realities of violence. Forgiveness as the act of willing the well-being of the other is a direct intervention that has the power to break the cycle of violence.

If forgiveness does not necessarily require warm feelings toward the violators, it also does not necessarily involve accepting violators into one's physical space. Indeed, the action of willing well-being toward victims as well as violators may well preclude such acceptance. The well-being of a child who suffers severe abuse from an adult might require physical and/or emotional distance or possibly rejection of the violator, even after the child reaches maturity. Similarly, the well-being of the violator may also require physical distance from persons the violator might be tempted to abuse. When experience has shown that the other cannot be trusted, forgiveness is not denial of this harsh reality, but an open recognition of this misfortune. Furthermore, often the after-effects of violation require the protection of psychic vulnerability through physical distance. Thus if the victim's acceptance of the violator is necessary for forgiveness, then it would be impossible for some victims ever to experience the release offered by forgiveness. But if willing the other's well-being does not require total acceptance of the other, there is no necessary contradiction between willing the violator's well-being and maintaining a vigilant caution toward that violator. Forgiveness necessarily requires the will toward well-being; it does not necessitate acceptance, and may in fact preclude it. Forgiveness construed as acceptance can continue to wreak ill-being on victim and violator; forgiveness as willing the well-being of the other takes account of the role of distance in well-being, and can therefore break the chain of violence.

The fact that forgiveness does not *necessitate* either loving feelings or acceptance does not mean that these factors are not possible within the act of forgiveness: to the contrary. Forgiveness is an event that spans time; it is not an all-at-once happening. Since forgiveness is the ground of transformation, it may be that the event of forgiveness will contribute to a change in the circumstances of the violator as well as the victim, making warm feelings or acceptance possible. Also, the will toward well-being that begins as a deliberate act of will may lead to affective feelings consistent with that will. And in less severe cases of sin within friendships and families, a generosity of spirit can accompany this will toward well-being, issuing in warmth and acceptance toward the other. But forgiveness must not be enmeshed in any essential way to these qualities, as if forgiveness could not be forgiveness without them. The primacy of forgiveness as an act of will insures that forgiveness and its concomitant release are possible even when the valued qualities of warmth and acceptance are not authentically viable.

The importance of forgiveness as an act of will involves not only the reality that in many cases the severity of sin and the remembrance of sin preclude emotional warmth and acceptance. The primacy of the will relates as well to that aspect of our distinctive humanity that evolves through self-transcendence as memory, empathy, and imagination. Empathy, as defined earlier in chapter two, involves recognition of the other as subjective other in relation to the self. Empathy is the de-absolutization of the self and therefore the transcendence of the self by knowing the self as one center among many centers, participating in a universe of centerless centering. Empathy requires a "feeling-with" that mediates the sense of interconnectedness; action based on that connectedness can be directed as ably by the will as by the emotions. And when emotions tend toward an absolutization of the violence endured, then the will alone serves as the severing wedge that breaks this absolutization by freeing the self through empathy. The will toward the other's well-being is the entry point into the self-transcendence of empathy that finally issues into the well-being of the self as well as the other in the wider community constituted as world.

To will well-being in response to violation cannot be confused with a "cheap grace" whereby persons do not have to deal with the consequences of their actions. On the contrary, well-being for a violator may involve coping with the rage and hatred within, learning how to forgive his or her own abusers, learning how to name one's guilt and forgive the self and others, learning how to reach out in caring. In short, well-being requires that the violator also must learn to exercise self-transcendence through memory, empathy, and imagination.

Well-being means transformation toward the good for both abuser and abused. The will toward well-being is not restricted to the violator, but necessarily includes the victim as well. This recognizes that for good or for ill, there is an entwining of victim and violator through the very nature of violation. The well-being of one is necessarily affected by the well-being of the other.

The most profound way in which this entwining occurs is in the after-effects of violation. Violence does not end with the completion of its occurrence; it insinuates itself into the ongoing experience of the victim. Violation amounts to the robbery of future time by forcing what should be new experiences to conform to the contours of the old. A person is robbed at gunpoint; the robbery happens in an instant. But does it? Does not the person live and relive the experience of the robbery, repeating the fear and anger in every unguarded moment? How many times does the litany of "if only" repeat itself? Insofar as the experience of violation invades our present time, it robs us of our future.

But the ghastly peculiarity of this aspect of violence is the sense in which the victim is joined to the violator. Violence lasts longer than the span of time occupied by its occurrence, since it repeats itself in the ongoing experience of the victim. Again and again the experience is relived. Yet the actual perpetrator of the violence is no longer present. Who, then, perpetuates the violence in the repeated cycles within the victim's psyche? In a major sense, of course, the violator is responsible, since the violator set this process in motion. But who continues the process?

In a relational world, there is a flow of feeling from one moment to the next, so that one's momentary constitution of the self is in part one's selective response to the events of the past. Traumatic violations have the power to overwhelm not only the past, but the present as well, interfering with normal selectivity. But no moment, no matter how traumatic, can of itself crowd out the novelty of the future. Every moment contains a potential for novelty that can break the grip of the past. When, then, one experiences the continuation in the present of a past violation, the past alone is not sufficient to account for that continuation. There is a sense, however small, in which the victim is also involved in maintaining the vitality of that violation through its continuation in the present.

This continuation of violence in the ongoing experience of the victim is the ultimate horror of violence, for the victim becomes the unwilling participant in his or her own victimization. Even though there is clearly a victim, and clearly a violator, in the ongoing experience there is a merging of the two. The violator, though perhaps no longer physically present, is made psychically present in the victim's continued revitalization of the crime in the psyche. This reality may be the vilest effect of violence, for in the worst case scenario, the victim comes to loathe the self insofar as it experiences itself as psychically joined to the violator.

To say that this effect of violence results in a "blame the victim" mentality is a gross reductionism. The point is not to establish blame, but to grasp the process of what in fact happens within the psyche of those who have experienced dire evil. The extensiveness of violence, through which it robs one of the freshness of time, is its power to ensnare the psyche of its victim. Violence may enter life in a moment, but it takes up residence in the hope of a lifetime lease. And if this happens with a single act of violence, the residual effects are reinforced a thousand-fold by continuing acts of violence, such as repeated incestuous relations or unremitting gang warfare or national warfare. The outward repetition of violence is more than matched by inward repetitions driven by screaming memories that insist upon their due. And their due is the victim's repeated reliving of violence, making the violator present even when physically absent. Victim and violator become melded into one.

Forgiveness as willing the well-being of violator *and* victim is essential if this internal effect of violence through time is to be broken. To will one's own well-being is to will that the violence be relegated to past as objective memory, no longer to be continued in the subjective experience of the present. A degree of novelty and freedom, even if minute, is inescapably a part of every moment, and it can be sufficient to break the continuity of violence. One can will one's well-being.

Part of the difficulty of entering into forgiveness, despite the transformation it offers, is the enormous sense of violation that insists upon retribution or restitution. And this sense of violation presents a subtle distortion to one's view, for it presents the world as if it were divided into victims and violators. I have already addressed the sense in which this division breaks down through the conjoining of victim and violator in the internalization of violence. But there is another sense in which it breaks down, and that is through the very pervasiveness of original sin as developed in chapters five through seven. To break the world cleanly into victims and violators ignores the depths of each person's participation in cultural sin. There simply are no innocents.

There is an ancient prayer in the Christian tradition that includes the petition, "forgive us our sins, as we forgive those who sin against us." The supposition of the petition is that forgiveness does not divide the world into the guilty and the innocent, but that the world is a community that is called to live from and in forgiveness given and forgiveness received. Even though the degree of guilt is variable, depending upon one's freedom and one's possibilities, there is no one who does not bear some degree of responsibility for what he or she has done with the inherited past, no one who does not in some sense integrate the sins of others into the self through solidarity, no one who does not experience an inherent inclination toward aggression that itself entails a capacity for violence. We are all caught in the chain of sin, and that chain can bind us like the chains around dead Marley's ghost in Dickens' tale. But the very openness to forgive another is at the same time an openness to receive forgiveness as well. And when forgiveness is hard to give—or to receive—the knowledge that neither the self nor others are excepted from the universal condition of sin as violence can open us toward the forgiveness that is our own as well as the other's release.

To will the well-being of both victim and violator requires that one reckon fully with the nature of the violation in the mode of transformation rather than repetition. To be caught in the continuous repetition of violence within the psyche distorts memory, for it is a vivid making-present of the past as if it were *not* past, but still present. Transformative memory is that remembrance of the past as *past*, opening one to a new present. It does not eliminate the continuing pain of loss set in motion by the violation, for release cannot undo the past. However, transformative memory can allow the past to *be* past for the sake of well-being.

The will toward well-being must be in the context of the fullest possible recognition of the sin, and therefore of the character of the violator. To attempt to "forgive and forget" is to blind oneself to the nature of the one needing forgiveness, thus turning forgiveness into mere sentimentality. Forgetting or ignoring violations has no place in the hard reality of forgiveness. Forgiveness involves contextual knowledge, not forgetfulness, since forgiveness requires that one actively and thoughtfully will the well-being of particular persons who are dealing with particular problems. Generic forgiveness is meaningless, given the specificity of violence.

Remembrance of violation does not reduce the violator to the violation, as if there were no other elements to her or his personhood. The world of relationality is far too complex to reduce any person to one set of relationships. Nonetheless, the relationship of violation is a constituent aspect of the violator, and to ignore this is to will the well-being of a construal of fantasy rather than a real person. One must will the well-being of victim(s) and violator(s) in the fullest possible knowing of the nature of the violation.

Nor is "love the sinner, hate the sin" an appropriate response when one dares to recognize the pervasive extent of the wrong. In a relational world it is not possible to separate a person from interactions with others. Who we are is a result of how we respond to our relationships in light of future possibilities. Violence is one way of responding to relationships, and when we choose to respond violently, we *become* that violent response: it is not separate from ourselves. If it were, we would try deeds in courtrooms, and not people. The one who robs is robber, the one who rapes is rapist, the one who murders is murderer, the one who maligns on the basis of racial qualities is racist. While it is reductionistic to pretend that a person is *only* robber, or rapist, or murderer, or racist, it is equally misguided to pretend that such actions are only external to the self and not a constitutive part of the self. And if we are to forgive others by willing their well-being, it will not do to will the well-being of a generic other; it is this specific other, the violator, toward whom one wills well-being. To attempt to "love the sinner but hate the sin," then, is to love an abstraction.

Note, however, the qualification of knowledge. The definition calls for the fullest possible knowledge; in no case is an exhaustive knowledge of any violation possible. Everything affects everything else in a relational world, and one cannot know the multiple effects of any event beyond oneself. Furthermore, individuals are sufficiently complex that there is no guarantee that victims or violators know the fullness of the effects of any violation even within their own selves. And just as one cannot know the nature of a violation and its effects exhaustively, neither can one know the factors leading into the violation exhaustively. Thus while forgiveness means that we must recognize the nature of sin, there are limits as to how fully the sin can actually be known. What forgiveness requires is that we will the well-being of victim(s) and violator(s) in the fullest knowledge of the nature of the violation that is currently *possible*.

Remembrance of sin in the context of forgiveness is quite different from remembrance of sin in the context of vengeance. The critical difference is the will toward well-being or ill-being. In the case of forgiveness, one remembers in order to transform; in the case of the vengeance, one remembers in order to destroy. Transformation involves hope for a new future, whereas destruction perpetuates the violence of the past, seeking to change only the roles of victim and violator. Memory is involved in the mode of transcendence in the one case, and in the mode of imprisonment in the other. Therefore while forgiveness cannot involve disregarding the violation, neither can it become entrapment in the memory of violation. It is memory in the mode of self-transcendence, integrating the memory into whatever new futures are yet possible.

Forgiveness is not always other-directed; it must also be self-directed. One of the ways of getting mired in guilt so that we do not move beyond it is by forcing self-directed guilt to loom so large that it shuts out all alternatives. To do this, of course, is to make guilt synonymous with the self, crowding out and stunting the holistic richness of what one can be. The tyranny of guilt narrows the current experience of the self by absolutizing one event of the self, one set of relations, one form of response. Relational existence is blotted out, as if in fact only the guilt of oneself mattered.

Accepting the will toward one's own well-being, whether from others or from the self, creates the dilemma of the loss of the guilty self one has internalized as one's identity. If that self is forgiven, who is the self to be? So the odd nature of the refusal of forgiveness is not only the absolutization of a past self, and the distortion of each successive present to fit the constricted parameters of that past, but it is also the loss of the whole self in the context of its relationships. One cannot accept forgiveness as the will toward one's own well-being, because there is no "one" whose well-being can materialize—there is only the empty mask of guilt.

But forgiveness is the release from guilt that pours the water of life upon the atrophied self, making growth finally possible. One need not worry about leaving too much guilt behind—given the pervasiveness of original sin, there will always be enough guilt to go around. But guilt turned into a stopping place is little more than a variation on the theme of sin as violence, this time turned in on the self. A proper approach to guilt is to understand it as a transitional space that awaits the release of forgiveness and transformation. And in this interdependent world, willing one's own well-being is simultaneously willing the well-being of others, since one's own condition necessarily affects the well-being of others.

I have pointed out how the dimensions of transcendence are embedded within forgiveness. Through the transcendence of memory, one differentiates oneself from absorption into the past by allowing the past to be past. This also involves openness to reclaiming a fuller past that contextualizes violence. Through the transcendence of empathy, one gains the ability to separate self from other and to see the other as fully other, even in relation to the self. One is then free to will one's own well-being and the other's well-being. Through the transcendence of imagination, one receives release from the past through openness to a new future. In and through imagination, the will to well-being moves into visions of well-being, which themselves empower one to work toward well-being. Thus memory, empathy, and imagination are the means through which forgiveness exists, not simply as a release from sin, but as the movement into transformation.

Transformation flows from that aspect of the will toward well-being that is also hope for well-being. One hopes for that which has not yet been, drawing upon a future made tentatively possible through the very act of forgiveness. To hope for transformation is to transcend the present through the vision of a different future. Forgiveness as the active will toward well-being is the creation of a new human future, and thus forgiveness is the substance of human hope.

One might broadly conceive of personal violation in temporal terms, since it corrupts all our dimensions of time. In terms of the past, the violence in the past tends to consume all other aspects of an otherwise richly diverse history. There is a malignant power to violence whereby it absorbs and subordinates all other memories to its own, reducing the wholeness of the past to itself. In terms of the present, distortion takes place in two ways. First, of course, there is the actual experience of violation and violence, whereby we are *now* robbed—or rob others—of well-being. Second, there is the distortion of the present when one continues to suffer the effects of past violence. The past is made present through the continued suffering, and again, there is absence of well-being. In terms of the future, possibilities are limited by the nature of the violence suffered or perpetuated. What might be is altered by what has been and what is. The power of sin is its ability to span time, corrupting time until all our times be no more than commentaries on variations of violence.

The definition of forgiveness as willing the well-being of those involved in violation also involves temporality in a way that parallels sin. If sin corrupts our times, forgiveness redeems our times. If guilt stops time, forgiveness opens us to a new future, and therefore to time itself as healing and transformative. Forgiveness as the will toward well-being does not eliminate or dishonor pain. Rather, it releases pain to time, letting time do its work of gently leading us to transformation. The refusal of forgiveness, on the other hand, is also the refusal of time; it is the insistence that the horror remain fresh and perennially present.

Forgiveness is release of the violation to its place in the past; it is a release into time and the hope of transformation. The alternative will to vengeance is violation and violence yet again, repeating the interminable cycle inaugurated by the original violence. Even an attempt to pretend the violator does not exist, so that one wills nothing at all toward him or her, is to remain entrapped in the violence. It stops time at that point prior to the violence, when the act was unknown. But in fact the act happened, and has become part of the psyches of its victims. To attempt to will nothing at all toward the violator is to violate one's own experience. But to will well-being is to affirm experience and to be released for one's own healing. Through forgiveness, one is given back the honor of each day's newness.

Throughout this discussion, forgiveness has been discussed on a personal level, and indeed, we often consider forgiveness the most personal of experiences, since it touches us at our deepest places of woundedness. However, I have put forth the argument that sin is not only personal, but social; we begin our lives conditioned to norms of ill-being for those marginal to our own particular society. And if sin is social as well as personal, then a forgiveness that applies only to personal existence and not at all to social existence addresses but a part of the enormous scope of sin. But how does one forgive society?

Ordinarily, forgiveness between an individual and a society has been relegated to the courts of law and our penal system; there one learns what it is to "pay one's debt" to society. But if original sin in this new context is valid, then we all have a debt to pay. What does forgiveness mean relative to social evil? How does one forgive society and its institutions? How does one receive forgiveness for the social sins in which one participates?

The presenting sin mentioned at the beginning of this chapter involves corporate greed and a carelessness toward persons who are minorities in society, as if they were expendable components of a profit-making enterprise. Since the news account reports a carelessness about toxic chemicals in the workplace, there is no reason to suppose there is any care about those chemicals in waste facilities. And finally, the news account presupposes a background of immense personal poverty and exploitation. How does one "forgive" the complex of persons and institutions involved in these sins?

If forgiveness requires full recognition of the violation, then the acknowledgment of the conditions stated in the news report must be supplemented with acknowledgment of the whole society's participation in this situation. When we are dealing with original sin and its effects, we deal with depths of sin within the very structures of consciousness through which we formed our notions of self and society. This is not to negate the actual responsibility of those most closely connected with the events; it is to recognize one's own complicity, however passive, in that responsibility. And ownership of responsibility requires that one also seek ownership in transformation.

A model for social forgiveness and transformation may be found in some respects in self-help groups. Alcoholics, for instance, teach us that while they may indeed transcend the effects of their alcoholism, they can never escape the psychic structures of alcoholism that have become part of their identity. They are, then, "recovering alcoholics" to the end of their days.

Similarly, we cannot rip out our structures of consciousness and begin all over again. The mediation of original sin through the normative structures of consciousness inherited through our social institutions means that, like the alcoholic, we cannot divest ourselves of those structures. At best we can conscientiously recognize them and to that degree transcend them, so that we have the possibility of becoming "recovering sinners" of whatever kind.

Forgiveness relative to social ills, then, begins with recognition of the nature and the pervasiveness of those ills, particularly through the normativeness that sustains and perpetuates them from generation to generation. But forgiveness is more than recognizing and naming evil to the fullest possible extent, it is intentionally meeting this evil with the will toward well-being. How does one will the well-being of society? Does this not risk devolving into a sentimental idealism? For if we cannot rid ourselves of the structures that orient us toward sin, what does it mean to will well-being?

Social groupings become the means to address social ills. Initially this appears paradoxical, since all within the social group are tainted by the very ills they seek to address. But transcendence is applicable in its own way to groups simply because the group is formed as a subgroup within the larger society. As a subgroup, it is neither sheerly identical with the larger society, nor totally separate from it, and in this mediated position it gains a foothold of transcendence. This subgroup provides a reflexive structure for a corporate examination of the larger structures in which it is embedded.

Furthermore, as a subgroup it has a greater power to affect the larger society than does an individual, simply because the society as a whole is made up through the loose interconnection of many groups. Social forgiveness, then, is the ability of those bonded together within a subgroup not only to examine the larger structures, but to influence the ever-fluid continuing formation of those structures. Society can no more deny its permeability by time than can the individual.

Social forgiveness as the will toward the well-being of victims and violators within society as a whole is formed through active participation in the transformation of society according to criteria of well-being. The ambiguity of this definition is not lost—that is, tainted norms are used to present visions of well-being, and often the visionary's reforming vision becomes the next generation's oppressive burden. Yet social forgiveness must be exercised through daring the actions of transformation, even while being willing to hold up one's visions and deeds to examination by those from different perspectives for critical evaluation. One participates in the transformation of society in and through the recognition that oneself is part of what needs transformation.

Social groups such as Amnesty International, Bread for the World, the American Red Cross, and countless churches become ways through which one can live out the implications of willing the well-being of victims and violators in North American society. The Base Christian Communities of Latin America offer yet another way. In these communities analysis of the social situation and analysis of one's social and spiritual resources form part of the activity of the community. But the basic power through which the community works is that Spirit generated in and through the intentional being-together of the community itself. The bonding of the Spirit and the knowledge of one's situation and resources are the catalysts whereby the community is a transforming agent for the well-being of the wider society, and the well-being of its own self.

Communities, like individuals, work through communal forms of memory, empathy, and imagination for the sake of transformation. Memory names the ills and the resources of the Spirit within the community and its surrounding culture. Empathy owns the subjectivity of the other; even the others who are over against one's good, so that one can genuinely will the transformation of the other into an agent of well-being. But communities particularly draw upon the transcendence of imagination to work the forgiveness that itself works the good of the wider society.

Communal imagination envisions a more complete well-being than is actually realized in the present sinful world. For example, judging racism as wrong is to call upon a vision in which society rejoices in diversity of race, and is so structured that the diversity contributes to the well-being of the whole, and therefore to the individual participants in that whole. To say it is wrong that only persons with sufficient wealth may receive adequate health care is to call upon a vision of a society where all have access to the means for healthy living. To condemn all needless violence, whether racism, sexism, classism, heterosexism or greed, or abuse, or warfare, or worker exploitation, or whatever form, is to envision a society governed by peace and well-being. There will be variations in the visions and competition among visions, but the point is not that there is one single vision of a better way, but that *some such* vision is inherently operative within the very pronouncement of a social situation as sinful.

The problem of original sin is a corporate problem. It is individual only insofar as we participate in the whole society. We receive from the whole, and our own individual selves likewise contribute to the whole. We must appropriately think of ourselves, therefore, not simply as individuals, but as individuals-in-relation to the whole, or as individuals-in-community. Just as there are necessarily communal aspects of our existence in relation to sin, even so there are necessarily communal aspects of transformation. Insofar as through the naming of sin and the recognition of guilt we are called to transformations that approximate the vision of a more justly ordered well-being, then we must do so not as individuals, but as individuals-in-community. Forgiveness in the context of original sin must be social, working through community, for community.

The problem of original sin is enormous. Its manifestation is in poverty, political torture, abuse of self and others in ghastly proportions. As an individual, despite all our visions, we can do little against such massiveness. But in a relational world, we are individuals-in-community. If the corporate institutions to which we belong are implicated in the phenomenon of original sin, they are also heirs to the possibility for institutional transcendence and transformation. Communities and institutions can be far more effective against the problems of social sin, outgrowths of original sin, than can any individual acting alone. Singly, we can do little; together, we can do much. The naming of sin and the ownership of guilt is a task belonging to communities as well as to individuals. Communities that dare to name and own their participation in the social structures of sin are communities that are able to critique themselves, and therefore able to enter into the great work and the great hope of transformation.

To consider ourselves as individuals-in-community in relation to the whole requires that forgiveness ultimately be set in the context of God. The treatment in this chapter thus far has dealt solely from the point of view of the structures of transcendence given in finitude, and these are at the same time the structures of forgiveness and transformation. But in the earlier portions of this book I established that violence against any creature is also violence against God, since God co-experiences the suffering of the creature. Therefore, we stand in need of forgiveness not only from each other, but from God.

How does God forgive? If transcendence is essential to our own forgiveness, and transcendence is the capacity for memory, empathy, and imagination, how are these applicable to God? Can divine transcendence *also* be defined as memory, empathy, and imagination? If so, how are they involved in divine forgiveness?

In chapter four, I spoke of God's truth, love, and beauty as together forming a criterion of well-being. What remains is to show that God's truth, love, and beauty are not only analogous to memory, empathy, and imagination, but are in fact the fullest possible forms of memory, empathy, and imagination. Forgiveness as an act of will involves knowledge, or memory of the violation; it involves empathy, or a will toward the well-being of victim and violator, and it involves imagination, or a will toward a well-being that is not yet achieved. God, as the fullness of truth, love, and beauty is memory, empathy, and imagination carried to maximal form. In God the criterion of well-being (truth, love, and beauty), and the elements that make for forgiveness (memory, empathy, and imagination) merge, so that in a sense one might say that the divine character *is* forgiveness.

With regard to the convergence of memory and truth in God, God is one and everlasting, and therefore there is no past for God. Yet if God is one, and God is ever receiving the world and transforming it into the well-being of the divine reality, then there is a sense in which all that has ever been still *is* in God. God does not have "a" past—but God contains "the" past. In this case, God has no "memory," for memory indicates a pastness that is recalled into present knowing. But God has "truth" in the sense of the fullest possible knowledge of all that has ever been. Truth in God would function analogously to memory for us. Like memory, it relates to the past, but to a past that is made present through its everlasting presence in God's own life. In God, memory and truth would be the same reality.

A similar dynamic would take place with regard to the convergence of empathy and love. Empathy feels the otherness of the other—but so, of course, does love. In God, the dynamic is intensified, if indeed God (as was argued in chapter four) resurrects the world into the divine life. Each element of the world would be recontextualized in God, being fully itself (since God feels it in its entirety), and yet a participant in God, who contains and sustains it. Otherness and sameness dance in the interchange between God and a resurrected world. In God, empathy and love converge.

The same is so with beauty and imagination. God receives the world into the divine self with a will toward the world's well-being, both in history and within the divine life. With regard to history, that which *can* be given to the world in all its particularity reflects God's beauty to a greater or lesser degree, depending upon the limitations of history. But within God, there is no limitation upon the well-being that God can fashion in the transformation of the world. This suggests that all of God's actions take place according to God's own ultimate vision of what can be, even within God's own self given the divine reception of *this* particular world. If imagination is a vision of that which is not yet, then God's transforming power is an ultimate form of imagination. And the imagination of God is an ever-changing vision of beauty wherein all manner of things shall be well. In God, imagination and beauty are one.

Since God everlastingly receives the world, God's will toward the world's well-being is a love that is also an acceptance. In our finite situation, acceptance and feelings of love are not always possible relative to those who violate others or ourselves. Often we simply cannot afford the vulnerability of acceptance and love, given the power of the violator over us; what remains for us is to will well-being. But God shows no such limitation. Rather, all violators, including ourselves, are invited into the great transformation that is God. In this transformation, the co-experiencing whereby God feels the world with us can become a co-experiencing whereby we feel the world with God. God's love is an ultimate empathy, of which ours is but a dim reflection. We are invited into the divine love that is finally God's forgiveness, God's own will toward our well-being. This opens us to the great possibility of sharing in God's love for the world, a love that extends even toward those who violate us.

Memory, empathy, and imagination are the components of forgiveness. Their analogues in God are truth, love, and beauty. But the vision of God is not simply that God *contains* truth, love, and beauty, but that God *is* the living activity of truth, love, and beauty. If this is so, God *is* forgiveness, not as an abstraction from our own, but as the ground of our own and as the lure toward our own modes of forgiveness. To forgive is to participate in the nature of God. And God's forgiveness of us is God's acceptance of ourselves toward the end of our transformation as individuals in an ever-enlarging community. Ultimately, that community is the reconciliation of all things, beyond all sin, within God's own self.

There is a vision that informs us. The vision is drawn from the whole universe of relations, and it bespeaks the beauty of reciprocal well-being, of justice, of love without boundaries. It bespeaks a vision of no less than the community of God. This vision calls us to recognize who we are individually and communally, and to live toward the hope of transformation. This hope is itself mediated through the peculiar togetherness of memory, empathy, and imagination. It brings intuitions of the well-being of earth and its inhabitants, luring us away from violence and toward transformation. The vision is brought ever to fruition through the divine and human event of forgiveness.

Conclusion

M y concern throughout this book has been to uncover some explanation of why it is that we humans are so capable of such great harm to all of creation, including ourselves. How is the horror possible that humans can and do delight in causing pain? My investigation has been primarily (though not exclusively) in the mode of natural theology, looking for answers not in Christian dogmatics, but in what appear to me to be the structures of human existence. I am quite aware, as my teacher John B. Cobb, Jr. noted long ago in *A Christian Natural Theology*,[1] that so-called natural theology is developed through questions and perceptions already shaped by the traditional categories of Christian thought. Thus the careful reader will notice an implicit Christology and doctrine of the cross in chapter 6, and an implicit ecclesiology in chapter 7. To the degree that these doctrinal implications are not developed, there is a certain incompleteness to the investigation. Nonetheless, as an exercise in a Christian natural theology, I have brought my task to its completion.

I have sought to lay out the theological foundations for a contemporary reappropriation of the doctrine of original sin. Original sin itself describes the human condition in which we find ourselves; it is the stage upon which we play out the drama of our human lives. I have defined this stage not in traditional terms of "rebellion against God," but in the more direct terms, "rebellion against creation." Sin is always an act that attacks creaturely well-being. The drive-by murderer may or may not have an intent to take God's place, but the drive-by murderer always has an intent to destroy the well-being of another person, whether carelessly or deliberately.

---

[1] John B. Cobb, Jr., *A Christian Natural Theology* (Philadelphia: Westminster Press, 1965).

The same might be said of the rapist, the racist, the bigot, the cheat, and the less dramatic sinner of daily life. Sin is a direct assault on the well-being of some aspect of creation.

Because God relates intimately to creation, experiencing its full realities, all sins against creation are also against God. God is the co-sufferer in every event of sin. Therefore, all sins that are directly against creation are indirectly against God. Reinhold Niebuhr expressed a similar insight when he said that rebellion against God is the religious dimension of every act of sin, but the ground of his statement was rooted in the supposition that humankind itself is in a situation of rebellion against God. Rebellion against God, he claimed, constitutes humans as sinners, so that acts against creation follow as a result of the primal rebellion against God. My own interpretation is that humankind is in rebellion against the fullness of well-being for creation, and that acts against God follow indirectly as a result of this primal rebellion against creation. Rebellion against creation constitutes humans as sinners, and even God feels the effects.

The tradition accounted for human sinfulness within the human will. The rebellion against God happens through misuse of human freedom, both primordially and in every human individual. Ancient theologians described the structure of sin through the story of Adam; twentieth-century theologians described the structure of sin through psychology as a condition of anxiety in the face of human finitude. In either case, trusting God was considered the antidote to anxiety and the prevention of sin. Instead, humans misused their freedom by choosing finite goods in a futile attempt to gainsay human limitations. The condition defines the parameters within which all human beings begin and live out their lives; hence it is "original" sin.

My theological shift to sin as rebellion against creation leads me to look within the conditions of creation for the structures that predispose us all toward sin. I find these structures not so much in human freedom as in human finitude. First, we are creatures with a bent toward aggression that easily leads to intents and acts of violence. Violence works the ill-being of some aspects of creation in the name of the well-being of the perpetrators of violence. Violence is the defiance of mutual well-being, and is a consequence of the competitive nature of existence in a world where "life is robbery." The bent toward aggression that is exercised through violence is an essential aspect of the structure of sin.

The second aspect of sin's structure follows from the interrelational nature of creaturely existence. Like a web that reverberates throughout its entirety in response to even the least disturbance, life mediates the violence experienced anywhere throughout its whole network. Our human sensory system screens most of the relational data of existence from our consciousness, but it cannot totally negate that data. Like the computer network that retains traces of deleted data, the human consciousness is a superstructure that retains the substructure of negated violence. Violence, not mortality, is the source of the anxiety that lies just beyond the edges of human consciousness. Proximity to violence pushes anxiety into awareness. Whether experienced consciously or subconsciously, anxiety over violence combines with our own individual bent toward violence, increasing the probability of sin.

The third aspect of sin is the formation of conscience through social structures that presuppose the ill-being of some for the sake of the well-being of those whose interests have created the structures. Social institutions are complex structures whose patterns of behavior have been rigorously analyzed by various experts. I have not attempted to repeat those analyses here. Instead, I have looked at another facet of institutional life, which is the organic intersubjectivity created through its relational structure. This intersubjectivity operates through the intensification of the missional purpose of the organization in something like a "hall of mirrors" phenomenon. Each individual connected with the organization internalizes the organization's purposes from her or his own perspective, and reflects that internalization back to the organization as a whole. There is therefore a multiple effectiveness to the organization that surpasses the effectiveness of any individual within society. Within the organization, this multiple purposiveness creates the unique ethos of the institution. Beyond the organization, the ethos is projected not simply through the institution's advertising or self-projection in society, but also through the participating individuals who carry their own peculiar internalization of the institution's purposes into their own influential living.

The same dynamic happens through all the institutions of a society, which in turn creates a culture. This culture is the complex expression of the convergence or contrast of the various goals of its constituent parts. It is the matrix of the society, shaping the contours of values and norms for every individual affected by that society, particularly children. Individual consciences are shaped through institutional values as mediated throughout the culture through language, art, and education. Conscience reflects culture. It therefore reflects the normative patterns of value that perpetuate the well-being of the institutions that form the culture. Insofar as the culture perpetuates norms of well-being for some at the expense of others, to that degree the culture sanctions the ill-being of those others. Conscience, then, is corrupted from its earliest formation. This factor, when combined with the substructure of anxiety/violence and with the inbred bent to aggression and violence, completes the threefold structure of original sin.

It is appropriate to call this substructure original sin because like the ancient understanding it describes a situation in which we become sinners without our consent. By the time one is capable of questioning one's involvement in ill-being, one is by definition already involved. The question is not whether one will sin, but how, when, and where. If the theological dimension of sin is that sin is rebellion against creation exercised through violence, then the structure of sin tragically guarantees that every human being will participate in this rebellion. Sinners will sin.

Yet sin is a salvific word, a word of grace. Sin can only be named as such when there is the possibility not simply of judgment, but of forgiveness and transformation. The naming of sin bespeaks a vision where violence is not the norm; it bespeaks transcendence through imagination of a new and different future. Such a vision measures sin, and the distance created by the measure is guilt.

Guilt is also a word of grace. To experience guilt for one's participation in sin is already to be removed from total immersion in sin. Guilt already whispers of transcendence over sin through a readiness to let the sin be past, and no longer present. As such, guilt is a transitional reality, inspired by the vision of an alternative future that requires the relinquishment of sin into the past.

And so the transcendence of future and past that is mediated by the confession of sin and the experience of guilt is at the same time an invitation to a new present of empathy with all creation. The result is forgiveness: the will toward well-being for both victim and violator in the fullest possible knowledge of the nature of the violation.

The peculiarity obtains, then, in an echo of traditional theologies, that to be human is to be caught in the structure of original sin. By definition, the condition of original sin marks our days and our ways, but we are nonetheless called and empowered to live from, in,

and toward the forgiveness of sins. We can be "recovering sinners."
Through forgiveness, we can receive, will, and act toward the well-
being of creation. By the grace of God, sin notwithstanding, it is yet
possible that all shall be well, and all shall be well, and all manner
of things shall be well.

Index